DIVING AND SNORKELING GUIDE TO

The Florida Keys

Second Edition

John Halas, Judy Halas

Don Kincaid

Pisces Books™

Copyright © 1993 by Lonely Planet Publications
Head Office: PO Box 617, Hawthorn, Vic 3122, Australia
Branches: 150 Linden St, Oakland, CA 94607, USA
                   10a Spring Place, London NW5 3BH, UK
                   71 bis rue du Cardinal Lemoine, 75005 Paris, France

Library of Congress Cataloging-in-Publication Data

Halas, John.
     Diving and snorkeling guide to the Florida Keys / by John and Judy Halas, Don Kincaid—2nd ed.
         p.   cm.
     Includes index.
     ISBN 1-55992-055-6
     1. Skin diving—Florida—Florida Keys—Guidebooks. 2. Scuba diving—Florida—Florida Keys—Guidebooks. 3. Florida Keys (Fla.)—Guidebooks. 4. Marine biology—Florida—Florida Keys. I. Halas, Judy. II. Kincaid, Don. III. Pisces Books (Firm) IV. Title. V. Title: Florida Keys.
GV840.S78H26 1992
797.2'3'0975941—dc20   92-23932
                                                                                 CIP

Printed in Hong Kong

Table of Contents

How to Use this Guide

No matter what kind of diver you are, a trip to the Florida Keys will be one of the highlights of your diving memories. These little islands, some not much higher than 2 feet (60 cm) above sea level and the highest about 18 feet (6 m), average less than a half mile (1 km) in width. Lying just offshore are the most beautiful underwater playgrounds in the United States. These tropical coral reefs extend from a point off the southern tip of the mainland and sweep south and west for 150 miles, (240 km) beyond Key West to the western limits of the keys.

The Rating System for Divers and Dives

Our suggestions as to the minimum level of expertise required for any given dive should be taken in a conservative sense, keeping in mind the old adage about there being old divers and bold divers, but few old bold divers. We consider a *novice* to be someone in decent physical condition, who has recently completed a basic certification diving course, or a certified diver who has not been diving recently or who has no experience in similar waters. We consider an *intermediate* to be a certified diver in excellent physical condition who has been diving actively for at least a year following a basic course, and who has been diving recently in similar waters. We consider an *advanced* diver to be someone who has completed an advanced certification diving course, has been diving recently in similar waters, and is in excellent physical condition. You will have to decide if you are capable of making any particular dive, depending on your level of training, recent experience, and physical condition, as well as water conditions at the site. Remember that water conditions can change at any time, even during a dive.

◀ *The Christ of the Deep Statue at Key Largo Dry Rocks was the gift of Italian, Egidi Cressi. It was placed by the Underwater Society of America and dedicated to "all who lived for the sea." (Photo: J. Halas.)*

1

Overview of the Florida Keys

Long ago, the Florida Keys were coral patch reefs awash in the tropical waters of the warm southern sea. In time, the waters fell and the coral reefs were exposed to the sun and the winds. Offshore more corals formed and were, in turn, broken down by the sea. Finally, the exposed coral islands gained an identity and became known first as Los Martires and later as the Florida Keys.

Human beings came and peopled the shores of the islands, and though life was hard, vegetation sparse, and water scarce, the sea provided abundant provisions. The Calusa Indians settled in villages in the Keys until they were victimized by the Spanish slavers and new diseases from another world. The Spanish were the next to leave their heritage with the little islands they called cayos. These colonists were dedicated to removing all the treasures of the New World and carrying them back to Spain.

Their fleets of large merchant ships, laden with riches and protected by large armed galleons, sailed regularly from Havana northward through the Florida Straits just offshore of the Florida Keys. These ships, borne by the prevailing southeast winds, made Spain the richest and most powerful country in Europe. Yet the sea was never predictable and the violence of a fierce tropical storm could rise without warning, driving ships inshore, ripping out the bottoms of the vessels, and strewing their contents over the sands and coral. Today, divers can still encounter the remains of ships of many countries driven into the shallows by hurricane winds or careless handling.

After the transfer of Spanish Florida to the United States in 1821, more and more people filtered into the Keys and commenced to make a home out of this ocean wilderness. They began an island trade and many of the Keys seafarers became "wreckers," salvaging the ill-fated vessels that were lost on the reef. Many assisted in rescuing men, ships, and cargo and the wreckers became the first Coast Guard of the Keys.

The power of the wind is still as popular a way to get around in the Keys as it was in the 16th, 17th, and 18th centuries, when ships of the Spanish Plate Fleets, carrying gold and other treasures, regularly sailed these waters. Many of those ships wound up on area reefs. Their cannons, anchors and ballast rock can still be seen by divers. (Photo: S. Blount.) ▶

Around the turn of the century, Henry Flagler extended his dream and built a railroad to the end of the Keys. Completed in 1912, the railroad was destroyed in the great hurricane of 1935. It was replaced by the Overseas Highway which used its embankment and bridges as the foundation for the roadway. Small green milemarkers along the road measure the distance from Key West and are used to note most locations in the Keys.

The Keys Today

The Florida Keys have been recognized as the "island diving you can drive to," and indeed it is true. The 135-mile (216 km) journey down through the coral islands and across the sparkling turquoise waters is one of the most beautiful in the United States. The highway leaves the densely populated mainland and visitors almost immediately enter a lonely stretch, inhabited only by birds and other wildlife, that separates the Keys from the rest of Florida. This expanse of mangrove and grassland swamp, essentially the same terrain that makes up the Everglades, ends at Jewfish Creek, first of the Florida Keys' many bridges and the acknowledged entrance to the Keys.

Upper Keys. Rounding the bend onto Key Largo, the largest of the Keys' islands, the Overseas Highway continues southward through a community of businesses, resorts, residences, signs, and vegetation punctuated with occasional structures that rise above the others. The proliferation of dive shops on Key Largo is immediately apparent as red and white "diver down" flags attract the many divers who visit the area. Key Largo has an excellent selection of resorts, motels, campgrounds, restaurants, fast food outlets, and stores catering to the diving public.

The town of Tavernier, on the southern end of Key Largo, has a shopping center with a movie theater and other businesses. Across the bridge is the residential community of Plantation Key. The local high school, the community hospital, and the sheriff's office, as well as several dive shops, are located in this area. Snake Creek bridge opens to permit tall vessels to pass through to either the Gulf waters or the Atlantic. More dive shops, restaurants, and the large resort of Holiday Isle are located on Windley Key. Centered at the next bridge, Whale Harbor, is a large fleet of charter boats. Islamorada, the "purple isle," stretches the length of Upper Matecumbe Key. This quaint town has many fine restaurants, established resorts, and a casual informal atmosphere all its own. Lower Matecumbe Key is generally a residential area with some resorts and a marina facility at its southern end.

Middle Keys. Channel Two and Channel Five Bridges span the waters where the Keys begin a gradual bend to the west. Below is the city of Layton and Long Key State Park. Long Key Bridge, the second longest in the Keys, essentially marks the transition point between the Upper and Middle Keys. South of here are the crowded commercial fishing community of Conch Key, the exclusively residential Duck Key, and the relatively sparse expanse of Grassy Key.

The center of Marathon, "the Heart of the Florida Keys," is at milemarker 50. This town features a full-sized air strip with daily commercial service from Miami. Many businesses are established here and a full range of services are available for visitors including a fully staffed community hospital. Marathon is also the location of the Highway Patrol and Sheriff's stations, the Middle Keys courthouse, high school, library, and other county agencies. Fishing and diving are prime attractions in this area.

Beyond Marathon lies the wide expanse of ocean spanned by the Seven Mile Bridge. Only slightly under seven miles, it is paralleled by the original bridge which still provides access to Pigeon Key. The upright posts and railings of the old bridge rate a careful look; they are made from the original rails of the railroad. From the vantage of the new bridge, it is easy to see the arches and footers of the bridge that became known as one of the wonders of the world. Off to the left, Sombrero Light stands its vigil more than five miles (8 km) out to sea.

This cannon once belonged to a British warship, the Winchester, *which sank near Carysfort Reef in 1695. (Photo: J. Halas.)*

5

Photographers will find excellent subjects, like this Spanish grunt on the Benwood, *when they dive the shipwrecks in the Keys. (Photo: J. Halas.)*

Three small keys, one devoted entirely to campers, lie between the Seven Mile Bridge and Bahia Honda Key. Bahia Honda State Park is located here and is well known for its swimming and camping facilities. This is also the headquarters for the Looe Key National Marine Sanctuary. A glance at the old Bahia Honda Bridge (visible on the left from the new bridge) leaves no doubt as to its original purpose as a railroad trestle. The new iron structure was too narrow to use as a roadbed, so the pavement was laid on top of the bridge!

Lower Keys. Farther down, past Spanish Harbor Keys, lies Big Pine Key, the largest of the Lower Keys and official home of the small key deer which sometimes browse for food along the roadways. The availability of fresh water, still obtainable from local wells, made habitation possible here and the island is a growing center of development.

Geologically the Lower Keys differ from those to the north. They are composed of Miami oolite, a sedimentary rock, rather than the limestone of the ancient reef formation. Generally, they lie perpendicular rather than parallel to the reefline. Closer to Key West, population increases. The Overseas Highway ends, or begins, at the Monroe County courthouse in the heart of Key West.

Key West is a unique blend of many cultures. Long ago, many Tory settlers from the Bahamas returned to Key West, sometimes bringing their homes with them piece by piece and reassembling them again. Some of these "conch houses" still stand today. These expatriates were called "Conchs" for the large pink mollusk which was their staple diet. A strong Cuban population has also added its cultural mix to the city.

Key West is truly a tropical paradise and boasts that it has never suffered a frost. The city offers the full range of services, accommodations, and amenities available in any town having an emphasis on tourist facilities and activities. To get to know Key West quickly, guided tours provide interesting and pertinent information.

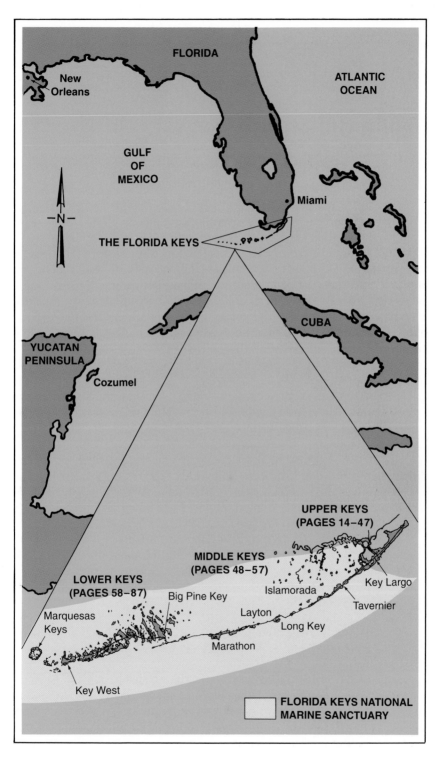

2

Diving the Florida Keys

Stretching the length of the Florida Keys about 6-7 miles (2 km) offshore, the fragile Florida Reef fringes the edge of the continental shelf. This reef system is the northern most living tropical coral reef in the continental United States. Thousands of minute delicate animals congregate in living, growing communities that have grown into the amazingly varied structures of stony corals and the gently waving plumes, branches, and fans of the soft corals. The beauty of this underwater world has lured many to venture beneath the clear blue waters of the Atlantic to explore and behold the wonders it reveals.

Island Shores. People who come to the Keys and want to sample the diving often ask where they can enter the water from the shore and see the coral reefs. Many are surprised to find that there are few actual reefs within swimming distance from shore. They also discover that there are no natural wide sandy beaches like those along the coast farther north. The island shores are fringed instead with mangroves, thick branching bushes that grow right out of the salt water. Their roots are like fingers that reach down and grasp the bottom to trap the debris which helps build the islands. In the water, hidden among these roots and branches, are small fish and other forms of sea life that take advantage of the offered protection until they are able to grow up and migrate to the sea.

Spreading out from the islands are the shallow flats, nursery grounds for the schools of juvenile fish that grow and populate the waters farther offshore. Without these safe havens, the schooling fish for which the Keys' reefs are known would not exist. Since few hard corals are found close to shore, the snorkeler who hopes to jump in the water and view the reef will find instead the fascination of a different world with rocks, mangrove channels, and grassy patches ready for exploration.

Patch Reefs. The first actual coral reefs occur about a mile or so offshore as patch reefs or underwater coral islands surrounded by grassy bottom. Here, flourishing soft corals and sea fans predominate, and these plant-like coral forms suggest the common name for these popular snorkeling areas, sea gardens.

Outer Reefs. The portion of the outer reef most commonly dived lies between 15 feet (5 m) and 35 feet (11 m). In this region of greatest relief, reef-building corals form "spurs and grooves," coral-covered limestone ridges and sand gullies that generally run toward the sea. This dynamic section of the reef, assaulted by storm waves and bathed by the Gulf Stream, provides an ideal habitat for marine organisms. A phenomenal variety of corals, fish, and other sea life thrive here and compete for space and food.

Above all, there is color. The hue of the water brightens the scene, and the spectacular brilliance of the tropical fish and the muted tones of the corals themselves blend in technicolor richness. A close-up look reveals a sprinkling of other vivid highlights — tube worms, sponges, anemones, crustaceans, and more. It is little wonder that this is the favorite area for most of the diving in the Keys.

Gulf Stream. All the features of the Keys, the islands, patch reefs, channels, and the outer reefs, run roughly parallel in a great arc sweeping from the west and bending to the north. They have been linked through time and influenced by the Gulf Stream, the great current that flows northward along the coast like a continuous river through the ocean. Gulf Stream water, which never falls below seventy degrees, bathes and feeds the reef corals and allows them to grow. Its crystal blue clarity allows warm clear diving all year in the Keys.

These divers remain well above the rounded star and brain coral colonies, being careful not to touch or damage these delicate reef-builders. (Photo: D. Kincaid.)

Fish of the Florida Keys

The beauty of the reef's sculpted forms is enhanced by the variety of fish weaving around varied coral colonies. Schools move and shift in unison and sometimes scatter to regroup again. Caribbean reefs cannot match this area in terms of the numbers of species and individual fish.

Patch reef areas commonly house small tropical fish. Many are juvenile species that are quite territorial and stay close to their own special habitat. The small French angel, basically black, has distinctive vertical yellow stripes. Small blue and gold-striped angels may grow up to be either queen or blue angels. Golden rock beauties have a black spot on their back sides which grows as they do. Finger-like yellow wrasses shepherded by blue supermales hang around the coral heads ready to perform their cleaning duties.

Probably the most common reef fish are the many species of striped grunts and snappers that crowd in large groups around the corals. Numerous incessant yellowtail snappers swimming swiftly past questing for tidbits of food should not be confused with goatfish, bottom feeders with barbels under their mouths. Gray or mangrove snapper are common and may be joined by mahogany snapper with purple trim on fins and tail, or dog snapper sporting a triangular patch under their eyes. Parrotfish of striking size and unusual colors examine the corals closely, often nipping at the rock with their beak-like mouths and releasing clouds of sandy excretion as they move along. Dark blue tangs in a unified mass move from one coral head to another past elongated trumpetfish, hanging suspended next to nearby features of the bottom. Butterflyfish, white and black and yellow, travel in pairs over the reef searching out their dinner.

Sharks, rarely seen in the Keys, should be respected but not feared by divers. The authors swam with three of these gray reef sharks for over an hour without any problem. The sharks were searching for a fish, hiding in the reef, which they had wounded earlier. (Photo: J. Halas.)

Often swimming singly, iridescent blue and green scrawl filefish glide by. Near the surface, small-mouthed Bermuda chub may search the floating sargassum weed for hidden morsels while schools of striped sergeant-majors and blue chromis swarm nearby.

Sharks and Barracuda. Most visitors to the Keys share a common concern about the fish they feel are "dangerous." Except for incidents associated with spearfishing, sharks or barracuda have rarely, if ever, bothered divers on the reef. Barracuda are common and appear menacing because they open and close their jaws as they breathe. Very curious about what is happening in their territory, they will follow divers and watch them closely, but swimming straight at a barracuda will usually cause him to move away. Sharks are seldom seen on the reef and local divers often feel it is a privilege to encounter one. As a rule, they pass quickly by, oblivious to people, searching only for real prey.

Getting to the Reef

Boat Rentals. People familiar with Keys diving are aware that the reefs in the Keys are really only accessible by boat and may choose to rent one. Divers who decide to rent should be competent boat handlers who know how to read charts well. Someone who has no knowledge of the local waters should probably not plan to use this means of getting to the reef. Novice divers should also keep in mind that there will be no expert available to put them on the good reefs and watch out for their safety.

Precautions. Captains are financially liable for any damage they may cause to the corals, either by grounding or anchoring. The anchor should always be set in the sand and the chain should be free of the surrounding bottom. Whenever possible, boaters should use the mooring buoys that have been placed along the reefline and are available to all.

Any boats with divers in the water are required by Florida law to fly the "diver down" flag, red with a diagonal white stripe, and many charter boats now also fly the internationally recognized "Alpha" flag, a double pennant of blue and white. Both flags warn other boaters of divers in the area. Divers should remain within one hundred feet (33 m) of their boats for these flags to serve their purpose. Boaters cruising through areas where there are divers should run at idle speed and look for divers' bubbles on the surface of the water.

Dive Charters. By far, the greatest majority of visiting divers in the Keys choose to leave the "driving" to the professionals who run the charter dive boats. Many dive shops in the Keys offer diverse charters that take people out to the most popular reef sites. Most of the time, snorkelers and scuba divers are together on the same trip, so families and groups of people who do not all dive can go together. Some shops, however, do separate the two types of diving or specialize in snorkel trips, taking snorkelers to shallower, more protected areas.

Any boat carrying passengers for hire must be run by a captain tested and licensed by the U. S. Coast Guard. Dive boats have varying capacities, but most shops have at least one boat certified to carry groups of twenty or more. Some shops may also have smaller boats that carry a maximum of six people. Charter operators in the Florida Keys maintain high professional standards of diving safety. Most carry crews trained in CPR, first aid, and the techniques of handling diving emergencies. Oxygen units and other safety equipment should be available on board. Responsible dive shops will readily explain their standards and safety practices.

Dive Requirements. When divers make arrangements to go on a charter, many dive shops in the Keys ask to see not only certification cards but dive logs as well in order to have a better idea about the experience of their passengers. Divers who have not been diving within the past year or who do not have a current logbook may be asked to go with a divemaster. Divers will be required to have a buoyancy compensator device, a pressure gauge, and equipment that is in good condition. Nearly every shop rents a full line of good quality rental equipment.

Divers without much familiarity with ocean diving should make sure that the sea conditions are suitable for their level of expertise before going on a charter. Divers on a Keys charter trip usually are not accompanied by a crew member as a divemaster, as they often are at Caribbean resorts. Because divers tend to spread out over the shallow reefs, captains watch everyone at the same time from the boat. Any problems, which are uncommon, tend to be handled more easily from the surface. People who are uncomfortable in the water on their own should look for shops that provide a divemaster as an extra service.

Deep Dives. More divers in the Keys are making deeper dives to the shipwrecks that have been sunk as artificial reefs. Most shops have very specific requirements for dives on these vessels. They may require advanced certification or a minimum number of logged open water dives with experience at deeper depths indicated. Again, divers that do not meet qualifications but want to dive the wrecks may arrange to go with a divemaster.

Current. The most important safety concern for divers in the Keys is the current. The effects of the Gulf Stream are not constant and the strength of the current varies as it meanders along according to the winds and tide. The outgoing tidal flow can also be strong. The currents are

"Bug hunting" means just one thing in the Keys, diving for the succulent spiny lobster. Check the game regulations in the area you plan to dive before taking any animal — fish, coral or shells. (Photo: J. Halas.)

deceptive. It is easy to be carried along with the flow and never notice the pull of the current until the time comes to swim back to the boat, low on air and energy. A diver in full scuba gear can have a very difficult time making progress with even a half-knot current. This is probably the most common diver safety problem for Keys divers and boat operators.

Underwater Hunting. Divers should be aware of the rules that govern the areas they dive. It is important to know what is protected and if there are limits to a catch. Taking any form of coral is illegal anywhere along the Florida reefs. The same is true for queen conch.

The Florida spiny lobster are protected during the closed season from April 1st through early August (the dates change often so consult the current laws.) During the open season, divers may take them by hand using nets or snares, but must avoid damage to the animal. Divers must have a lobster gauge with them in the water and should measure all lobster as they are caught. Undersized lobster and females bearing eggs may not be taken at any time. Severe penalties are in store for anyone molesting traps belonging to lobster fishermen.

Spearfishing is illegal within state waters — inside the 3 mile (4.8 km) limit — from Long Key north to Dade County. It is also not allowed near any public fishing piers or bridge catwalks. Spearfishing is especially prohibited within the protected areas of the Florida Keys National Marine Sanctuary.

Most of the marine life within these areas is protected. It is better to leave things undisturbed and follow the diver's maxim of "take only memories and leave only bubbles!"

13

3

Diving the Upper Keys

Sheltered by Key Largo, the largest of the Keys, the northernmost section of the reefline flourishes and some of the best developed reefs thrive here. Lush stands of magnificent elkhorn, huge mounds of star and brain corals, and shimmering soft corals are populated everywhere with myriads of fish and undersea creatures.

Marine Sanctuaries. In the late 1950s, concerned citizens recognized that this beautiful and priceless resource was threatened. The concept of an underwater park protecting the reefs gained momentum and by 1960, dedication ceremonies proclaimed the creation of the newest state park and the very first underwater marine park in the world, John Pennekamp Coral Reef State Park. By 1963, Pennekamp Park, located at milemarker 103, was opened to the public.

This magnificent undertaking protected a 25 mile (40 kilometer) stretch of reefline from beyond Carysfort Reef south to Molasses Reef and inshore to the coast line. But, in the mid-1970s, the Supreme Court restricted state waters to within the three-mile limit, which left the main reef line unprotected. Then, in 1975, the National Oceanic and Atmospheric Administration (NOAA) decided protection of the marine environment was a high priority and created the Key Largo National Marine Sanctuary just offshore of Pennekamp Park, safeguarding the reefs once more. Later, in 1981, the Looe Key National Marine Sanctuary in the Lower Keys was also added to the program.

In November 1990, in response to several grassroots private programs aimed at protecting the marine environment and spurred on by significant ship groundings on Florida reefs, Congress passed an act designating the Florida Keys National Marine Sanctuary. The new marine sanctuary is the nation's largest and stretches from Biscayne National Park south of Miami along the 300-foot depth line (99 m) as far as the Dry Tortugas. Waters on either side of the Keys are included encompassing the complete Florida Keys tropical marine ecosystem.

Snorkelers and divers can enjoy the many shallow coral areas all along the island chain. When water from the Gulf Stream moves in over the Key reefs, visibility can be extraordinary. (Photo: S. Blount.) ▶

Dive Site Ratings

Upper Keys

	Novice Diver	Novice Diver with Instructor or Divemaster	Intermediate Diver	Intermediate Diver with Instructor or Divemaster	Advanced Diver	Advanced Diver with Instructor or Divemaster
1. Carysfort Reef*	x	x	x	x	x	x
2. The Elbow*	x	x	x	x	x	x
3. Christ of the Deep Statue*	x	x	x	x	x	x
4. Grecian Rocks*	x	x	x	x	x	x
5. *Benwood* Wreck	x	x	x	x	x	x
6. French Reef*	x	x	x	x	x	x
7. White Bank Dry Rocks*	x	x	x	x	x	x
8. Molasses Reef*	x	x	x	x	x	x
9. U.S.C.G. *Duane* and *Bibb*				x	x	x
10. Pickles Reef*	x	x	x	x	x	x
11. Conch Reef*	x	x	x	x	x	x
12. Davis Reef*	x	x	x	x	x	x
13. Hen and Chickens*	x	x	x	x	x	x
14. The *Eagle*				x	x	x
15. Historic Shipwrecks: *El Infante, San Pedro,* and *The Alligator*	x	x	x	x	x	x

* Good snorkeling area

Key Largo. The dive shops of Key Largo and points south regularly dive the spectacular coral reefs offshore of this key. Traditionally, this is the area of the Key Largo National Marine Sanctuary and John Pennekamp Coral Reef State Park. Three important navigational lights stand as sentinels beckoning to those who seek the adventure of the underwater world. To the north is Carysfort Light, named for a British ship that grounded there in 1770. This reef light replaced the lightship in 1852 and now it is the oldest still-functioning lighthouse of its kind in the United States. The Elbow is the middle light and marks a distinct bend, or elbow, in the reefline. At the south end is Molasses Light. The tower rises above one of the most popular and beautiful reefs in the world. Throughout this area are scores of fascinating and varied dives, some well-known and others virtually unexplored.

Upper Keys. The shops from lower Key Largo to Islamorada generally dive the reefs south of Molasses. Although dives often are in the 35 foot range (11 m), many of these shops offer trips to deeper waters. The addition of the deep wrecks used as artificial reefs have added a new dimension to diving here.

If you wish to make a special dive, call or write the shops well in advance of your arrival to determine when a trip will be scheduled. Weather affects dive plans as well, so be prepared for rescheduling.

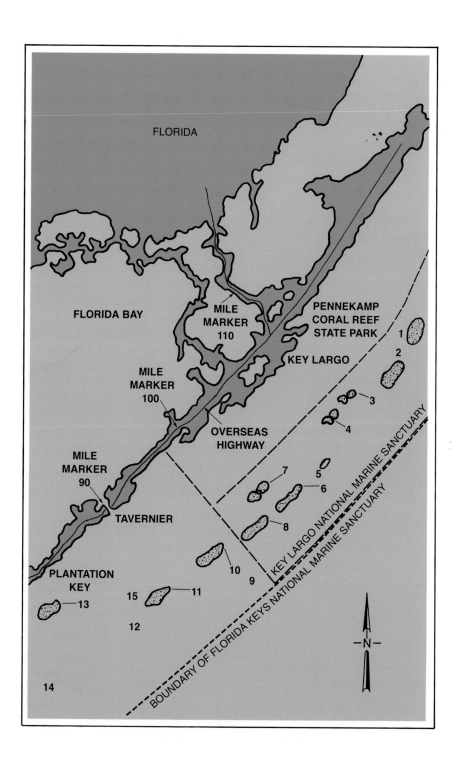

Typical Depth Range: 35-70 feet (11-21 m)
Typical Current Conditions: Variable (none to moderate)
Expertise Required: Intermediate
Access: Boat

At the north end of the marine sanctuary, historic Carysfort Lighthouse marks the most remote regularly dived reef in the Upper Keys. The site derives its name, though changed, from the British ship, H.M.S. *Carysford*, which grounded here in 1770.

Most of the dive shops on the north end of Key Largo dive this reef, but it is usually a special trip rather than a regularly scheduled daily run. If you want to dive this area, it is best to check with various shops to find out when they plan to go. The one good factor about the relative inaccessibility of Carysfort Reef is that there is little boat traffic, even on busy holidays, so most of the time divers will have the reef to themselves.

The Gulf Stream swings offshore as it passes Carysfort Reef, so the northerly current occurs less often and is not usually strong in this area. However, tidal currents moving offshore can be tricky, and it is important to realize the effects of the current and that it can change during a dive.

Carysfort Reef has an unusual "double reef" configuration. There is a proliferation of shallow corals, perfect for snorkeling, quite near the light, but these thin out as the depth gradually increases. A limestone bottom, dusted with sand and covered with sparse sponges and soft corals, extends out to about 35 feet (11 m) where there is quite a steep drop down to 65 feet (20 m). Along this "near wall" is a lush growth of coral colonies. Platelike forms of *agaricia*, or lettuce coral, cascade down the reef face. At the base of the reef is a channel of fine sand, over 100 feet (33 m)

The shallow, sandy area behind Carysfort Reef is a beautiful, sheltered sandy anchorage. Many varieties of coral, including this stinging fire coral, grow right up to the surface of the water, and can be explored by snorkelers. (Photo: J. Halas.)

Photographers hoping to capture portraits of queen angels and other species should take care not to kick up the fine sediment at Carysfort Reef with their fins. (Photo: J. Halas.)

wide, that parallels the reef line. Across this sand channel, a second offshore reef rises back up to 35 feet (11 m) and then slopes down again on the far side.

To dive the reef face, plan to enter the water and swim offshore. Descend to the base of the reef at 65 feet (20 m) and begin exploring in either direction. If there is a current, swim against it along the front of the reefline. This is an intermediate dive because of the depth, and more inexperienced divers should be sure to monitor time and depth and return to the boat when conditions warrant. If there are any photographers in this area, take care not to stir up the fine sand on the bottom.

Near the light, divers may sometimes come across instruments, equipment, or markers associated with various reef research projects. Many of these are long-range studies that may take several years to complete. Although diving is not restricted here, scientists are hoping that people in the water will respect the importance of their work and not impair their efforts.

Other Dive Sites. To the south of Carysfort Light, a broad expanse of magnificent elkhorn coral forms Carysfort South, the largest shallow reef in the sanctuary. The reef appears flat as the corals have grown to the limit of the low tide. The backside is a calm haven for snorkelers. Offshore, massive star corals loom over a labyrinth of undercut ridges, gullies, and an occasional swim-through tunnel. Inshore is one of the area's finest snorkeling areas, Captain Tom's Wreck. Sunk here to provide shelter for fishermen, the *Charles W. Baird* burned to the waterline around 1940 when a camper lit a fire on her wooden deck. Farther down the reef line, Watson's Reef forms a horseshoe of fire coral around an old anchor. A deep cave, sheltering myriads of glass minnows, is the focus of thrilling action when large jacks and groupers swoop in and out of the cave entrances.

Typical Depth Range:	12-35 feet (4-11 m)
Typical Current Conditions:	Variable (none to strong)
Expertise Required:	Novice
Access:	Boat

When you look at a chart of the Upper Keys, it is easy to see that the Elbow is appropriately named. It juts out like a crooked arm as the reef doglegs to the north. The Elbow reef has been a catch-all for cargo ships, and its wrecks are the most notable feature of the area. The fish here, tamed by frequent feeding and plenty of attention, are responsive and certainly not camera shy. It often appears as if they enjoy posing.

Diving Wrecks. There are three major wrecks on the Elbow and each makes an interesting dive. Farthest north and offshore is a metal-hulled wreck, probably a steamer known as the *Tonawanda,* lost in 1866. There is not much relief to the structure, which has been bent and scattered. Just offshore of the tower, the wreck known by some as the *City of Washington,* a schooner lost here in 1917, has settled into the sands and is now manned by a crew of lively fish. The Civil War Wreck, an older

The remains of a wooden Civil War era wreck attracts a variety of fish at The Elbow, where the Key Largo reefs curve to the southwest. (Photo: J. Halas.)

Cannons and anchors don't always mark the site of a wreck. When sailing ships ran aground, their crews often tried to refloat them by lightening the vessel. Heavy metal objects, such as this heavily encrusted cannon, were normally the first things overboard. (Photo: J. Halas.)

shipwreck with wooden beams and iron fasteners, lies just north of the tower. It is a place of isolated beauty sitting in a flat area of sand and grass. The wooden framework of the ship, held together with long iron pins, forms a great boxy structure where many fish weave in and out.

The most centralized dive spot is on the schooner, which has the most to offer a diver with a full tank. This is also the site of most of the fish-feeding activity, so there are lots of friendly fish about. Photographers like this wreck because the standing sides and walls of jutting jagged metal make unique silhouettes, and folded plates form hideaways for shy species. Look for the large green moray who lives here.

Other areas to examine extend out from the wreck. Beyond a coral ridge flanking the end of the ship nearest the light is a sand channel where larger grouper often wait until they can repossess their wreck from the divers. At the other end, the coral shelf drops off into more sandy areas where you may find the chain of giant links stretched across the reef. Along a sand channel inshore, is an old Spanish cannon left here long ago.

Elbow Fingers. Another shallow dive at the Elbow features coral ridges topped by giant elkhorn corals. The outstretched arms of these shallow water coral colonies reach toward the surface to provide habitat for schooling grunts and mixed snappers gathered under them. Lobster are commonly found under the low coral ledges in this area.

Typical Depth Range:	Shallow to 25 feet (8 m)
Typical Current Conditions:	Variable (none to moderate)
Expertise Required:	Novice
Access:	Boat

The figure of Christ stands silhouetted against the blue waters of the ocean. His arms, upraised to the surface, beckon to the multitudes to enter and be with Him. This dramatic and memorable picture is one that most diving visitors to the Keys will want to carry home with them.

Placed in a sand channel on the offshore side of Key Largo Dry Rocks, the statue sits in an amphitheater of corals near one of the most spectacular diving and snorkeling reefs of the Keys. On busy days, the statue is the hub of activity here as bubbles from many divers rise to tickle snorkelers peering down from the surface. Fish glide through the arms of the statue

The Christ Statue is one of the most famous of the Florida National Marine Sanctuary's attractions. Cast in bronze, the 9-foot (3 m) statue is located at Key Largo Dry Rocks. (Photo: J. Halas)

Resembling the convoluted form of the human brain, these rounded coral colonies are common on the Florida reefs. One of the most famous large brain corals is located near the Christ Statue. (Photo: J. Halas.)

and may stop to nibble on marine organisms growing there. The left hand points toward a massive rounded brain coral, famous for its size.

The statue area is perfect for beginning divers. Though shallow, less than 25 feet (8 m), a dive here is always interesting. Divers can work in either direction along the front edge of the reef, exploring the sand channels which run out from the center of the luxuriant coral growth. Snorkelers will be delighted with the prolific coral wonderland growing only a few feet below the surface. Vibrant colors dance and shimmer as the sparkling tropical fish move about the reef. Snorkelers should be reminded, though, in the very shallowest areas not to stand on or touch the corals.

On days with exceptional clarity, there may be a moderate current running, so divers should not go too far before checking the strength and direction of the flow. Because there is quite a bit of boat traffic here, divers need to surface carefully, staying close to shallow coral formations for protection.

The Christ Statue has become one of the most photographed underwater sites in the world. It is a popular spot for underwater weddings, some of which have been very creative and lavish. The statue itself was cast in Italy and donated to the Underwater Society of America by Egidi Cressi, an Italian industrialist. It is a 9 foot (3 m) tall bronze duplicate of the Christ of the Abysses statue, which stands in 50 feet (15 m) of water off Genoa, Italy.

Grecian Rocks 4

Typical Depth Range:	Shallow to 25 feet (8 m)
Typical Current Conditions:	Variable (none to moderate)
Expertise Required:	Novice
Access:	Boat

Grecian Rocks, a crescent-shaped patch, is an exceptionally popular reef for snorkelers. Grass and sand on the back side provide good anchorage and several mooring buoys are available. The shallow reef buffers the waves so the waters are very calm even on windy days. It is easy for snorkelers, even beginners, to swim from the boat up to the reefline where the corals and brightly colored fish abound.

In the back-reef area, the elkhorn and staghorn colonies rise from the rubble zone along the fringe of the coral thickets. Here lazy barracuda keep a watchful eye on their visitors, moving slowly out of the way when swimmers come near. Large star coral heads cluster close to the surface, tempting swimmers to stand on their surface for rest and a break. However, dive operators will quickly remind people not to harm these living animals in such a way. At high tide, swimmers can venture into the shallower areas where the corals nearly touch the surface, but need to take care that wave surge is not great enough to thrust them into the rocky colonies.

The north end of Grecian Rocks makes an enjoyable, though shallow, dive for scuba enthusiasts. The depth generally ranges from 15-20 feet (5-6 m) around the end and toward the front of the reef. Many big coral heads form a bulwark that protects the shallower region of the reef.

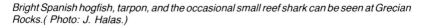

Bright Spanish hogfish, tarpon, and the occasional small reef shark can be seen at Grecian Rocks.(Photo: J. Halas.)

Snorkelers at Grecian Rocks can look for the cannon hidden in the star coral. Cannons are occasionally found in the waters of the Upper Keys. (Photo: J. Halas.)

Cannons in the Park

Every once in a while, divers and swimmers unexpectedly come across a legacy from the venturous warships of long ago-isolated cannons on the ocean floor.

Two such cannons are located on what is known as the Cannon Patch, a small patch reef along the route to Grecian Rocks. Like most iron objects which have been underwater for a long time, these are heavily encrusted with a thick coral-like coating of calcareous oxide. They almost appear to be made of stone, but the elongated shape is clear as they lay juxtaposed on the bottom. Nearby are fused cannonballs piled up amid the waving gorgonians and busy fish that pick away at their surface. There is no record left of how these cannons came to be in this place; the solution of the mystery is left to our imaginations.

Observant snorkelers at Grecian Rocks can find another old cannon within the central hollow of a large star coral head in the middle part of the back reef. This small cannon, found elsewhere in the park, was placed there years ago by the park rangers. At the Elbow, sitting in a sandy channel aimed at nothing, is another large encrusted cannon.

The *Benwood* Wreck   5

Typical Depth Range:	50 feet (15 m) offshore, 20 feet (6 m) inshore
Typical Current Conditions:	Variable (none to strong)
Expertise Required:	Novice to intermediate
Access:	Boat

The *Benwood* is an outstanding wreck dive and perfect for a novice diver. It is a large ship, easily accessible by boat, and it can be safely explored in a single dive. For those not used to dealing with the deceptive currents that tend to carry divers downstream, this wreck provides a focus. There is not much temptation to stray away from it because the bottom terrain is relatively barren in the surrounding area. The visibility is usually very good, but there is still plenty to see on days when it is less clear.

The wreck of the *Benwood* lies on the outer reef 1.5 miles (2.5 km) north of French Reef. Near midnight of April 9, 1942, this Norwegian freighter, sailing with no lights because of the danger from German submarines, was accidentally rammed by the *Robert C. Tuttle*. Turning toward shore, she went aground at the stern with her bow swung out to sea.

The ship lies with her bow in 45 feet (14 m) of water and her stern 300 feet (97 m) inshore at a depth of 25 feet (8 m). Begin a dive around the bow, which towers up from the bottom and makes a magnificent

The Benwood, *a modern steel wreck, has been broken into numerous pieces over the years. Its main attraction is the hordes of fish that swarm over the site. (Photo: J. Halas.)*

The Benwood *provides habitat for many large fish. Some, like this Nassau grouper, have become very friendly. (Photo: J. Halas.)*

backdrop for a photographic panorama. The marine life growing across the broad expanse of this flattened surface provides good subject matter for close-up or macro photography.

Experienced divers might enjoy swimming out a short distance along the ledge that runs offshore from the bow. About 100 feet (33 m) away in 50 feet (15 m) of water, the flukes of a large anchor much older than the *Benwood* rise from the sand next to the ledge.

There are many places on the ship where you can swim under or through the wreckage, but no real inside exploration is possible. If you venture into any of the openings in the hull or under the twisted plates, be careful. Remember those spaces look larger than they are, and dangling hoses are easily caught on the jutting steel.

Along the south side of the *Benwood,* look under the bottom of the hull for the moray eels, lobster, glassy sweepers and other fish that can be seen there. About midway along this side of the ship, you may want to venture out in the sand about 25 feet (8 m) to look for the jawfish that nest there. Rising above their burrows, they quickly drop back down tail-first when divers approach.

At the end of your dive, relocate your boat by looking up toward the surface. Because so many boats converge on this one popular place, boat traffic is very heavy here. Come up one of the buoy lines to the surface or try to ascend so you will come up near your dive platform and keep the current in mind, if it is present. If you are running a boat in the area, keep a careful lookout for divers approaching the surface and be extremely careful if you anchor. Watch the bubbles!

27

Typical Depth Range:	Shallow to 100 feet (1-33 m)
Typical Current Conditions:	Variable, often strong
Expertise Required:	Novice to advanced for deeper dives
Access:	Boat

The outstanding feature of French Reef is its caves. No other dive site in this area has so many swim-throughs, overhanging ledges, and actual caves than this lovely reef located 1.5 miles (2.5 km) north of Molasses Reef. These are not the kind of caves that require special equipment. Rather, they are 3-4 foot (1 m) high openings under the limestone rock that divers can peer into or swim through.

The secret to finding the exciting diving on French Reef is to be guided by the mooring buoys there. At the south end, is Hourglass Cave. Once inside, it is readily apparent how this was named. In the middle is a vertical limestone column shaped like an hourglass that divides the cave into two sections. Large grouper often hang out here.

Christmas Tree Cave is named for the large conical star coral mound that rises over the top. This is a swim-through passage about 4 feet (1.3 m) high with two entrances. The broadest opening is on the side toward the sandy bottom. On the other side, divers exit through an opening surrounded by corals. There is plenty of light and both openings can be seen at once. Divers should pull themselves through by hand rather than kicking up bottom sediments. Inside, look up at the ceiling of the cave where bubbles of trapped air shimmer silver reflections of light overlaying red, yellow, and gray spongy growths coating the rock.

Blackbar soldierfish prefer dark areas, such as the caves at French Reef. Divers should be very cautious in entering any of the passageways through the reef, as many are dead-end tunnels. (Photo: J. Halas.)

Southern stingrays may be found in the sand between the limestone spurs on French Reef. Divers approaching slowly can often get close but need to watch the stinging barb at the base of the tail. (Photo: J. Halas.)

From the wide sandy entrance to Christmas Tree Cave, across the sand patch is a limestone and coral "island" deeply undercut with crevices, recesses, and grottoes on the north side. Though it is tempting to penetrate and explore these, be careful because some of them are dead-end passages and some are a tight squeeze for divers with tanks. On the offshore end of this rocky formation, a large unnamed cave opens wide. It resembles the stage of a theater except the players are all fish.

Up the reef, a rounded opening breaches a reef wall leading into a large sandy patch. On its far side, White Sand Bottom Cave opens under a ledge and is home for many large fish. Swim through here and head offshore to the left where a buoy marks the entrance to a beautiful cave that is actually a long crevice. This is at the end of "Dog Snapper Ledge" where these large snapper with a distinct triangular patch under their eyes are commonly seen.

Beyond this area to the north is a shallower area of ridges covered with elkhorn corals and numerous fire coral ledges, a good place to look for lobster. The inshore side of this part of the reef has beautiful brain and star coral heads. One of these has grown right over an old galleon anchor whose flukes stick out from under the large head. The size of this coral indicates the long time since its loss.

A new system of drilling into the reef to attach mooring buoys has reduced damage to corals because of careless anchoring.

Mooring Buoys in the Florida Keys

At some of the most heavily dived reefs in the Florida Keys, mooring buoys have been installed to help reduce the damage inflicted on corals by carelessly placed anchors.

The key to these buoys lies in the way they are attached to the bottom. Unlike former buoy styles, these do not have large heavy chains and concrete bases (which cause as many problems as they solve) but rather are drilled directly into the limestone bottom and installed by cementing a stainless steel anchor pin into the 18-inch hole. The ring on the end is the only part that shows once this is completed. Attached to this is a thick yellow line that holds the large floating white mooring buoy, recognizable by its blue stripe. On the surface, boaters hook up to a pick-up line that trails in the water.

The first six mooring buoys of this kind were experimentally placed at French Reef in 1981. They were a success and the program, initiated by the Key Largo National Marine Sanctuary, has been expanded with the help of several non-profit organizations, the local communities, and both the state and federal governments. The buoy program will continue to grow to give the Florida Keys reefs additional protection.

Buoys are available to everyone without restriction. To attach to one properly, approach from down wind or current. Stop the boat when the pick-up line is near the bow. Using a boat hook, bring the loop at the end up to the boat and attach your own line through it. Pay out additional scope to reduce wear and add more resiliency to the buoy system. After you get in the water, inspect the system to make sure everything is in good condition.

Typical Depth Range:	Shallow to 25 feet (8 m)
Typical Current Conditions:	None to occasional
Expertise Required:	Novice
Access:	Boat

Boats on the way to French Reef must take care as they pass between two shallow patches known as White Bank Dry Rocks South and North. White Bank is an extensive sand bank that stretches north and south along the offshore reaches of Hawk Channel. Along its edge are numerous patch reefs and isolated coral heads which make excellent sites for snorkeling or fishing. White Bank Dry Rocks make up the largest of this area's lovely sea gardens.

Both of these twin patches are fine snorkeling spots with protected anchorages. They are prime examples of outer patch reef development with staghorn and elkhorn beds around the fringes. Small star and brain coral heads are scattered over the reef flat, and many spectacular species of gently surging soft corals produce a true garden effect.

Snorkeling in these patch reef areas comes close to swimming in an aquarium because the small tropical fish that collectors love to display commonly dwell here. Remember though, in this protected sanctuary, collecting of any sort is not allowed in order to ensure that these beautiful areas will be a legacy to the future.

Large elkhorn patches in shallow water make White Bank Dry Rocks appealing to divers and snorkelers. (Photo: J. Halas.)

Molasses Reef   8

Typical Depth Range: Shallow to 40 feet (12 m)
Typical Current Conditions: Strong northerly current usual
Expertise Required: Novice to intermediate
Access: Boat

Molasses Reef is generally considered to be the most popular reef in the Upper Keys and is possibly the most visited dive site in the world. The spectacular location lends itself to superlatives. Although it may have rivals for any one aspect, it really is deemed by many to have the most beautiful corals, the greatest relief, the most innumerable fish in the largest schools, and the clearest water.

This is a classic outer reef with a well-defined spur and groove system of coral development. The shallow coral ridges begin near the tower and stretch toward deeper water. At a depth around 35 feet (11 m), the massive corals terminate and a zone of low profile relief extends offshore to deeper water.

At the south end of Molasses Reef, mooring buoys are located near a ridge of corals which has an undercut cave on the south side. Several

Molasses Reef is famous for its many fish. Here squirrelfish and grunts crowd around a brain coral. (Photo: J. Halas.)

A ship's winch marks one of the outstanding dive areas of Molasses Reef, a large sandy basin surrounded by coral heads. (Photo J. Halas.)

permit, large silvery free-swimming fish with forked tails, are usually seen here constantly on the move around the reef. Just north of this is an old ship's anchor lying flat on the bottom. It is camouflaged by its encrustation and the attached corals and sponges which closely resemble the surrounding bedrock. There is no way to learn how this anchor, longer than the average person, came to rest in this place.

The Winch. The central portion of Molasses, squarely offshore of the light, is one of the most beautiful dives along this reef. Occasional wreckage is scattered throughout this area, but the most dramatic evidence of a ship's desolation is a lone winch or windlass that sits isolated in the center of a barren sandy patch where small barracuda commonly lie stacked up like motionless matchsticks. Directly inshore of the winch, a sand channel outlet leads toward the light. A short way along the ledge is a hole through the coral wall large enough to swim through and always populated by many milling fish. Under the ledge on the south side opposite the hole, a long green moray eel often stretches out, watching.

Seaward of the winch, a sand channel cuts between towering coral walls. In this ravine, the coral formations provide a thrilling backdrop for the shifting schools of various multicolored reef-dwelling fish. A maze of massive star coral heads sport their own decorations. Many colorful Christmas tree worms grow in vivid spirals that look like tiny flowers sprouting from the coral colonies.

The northern sector of Molasses Reef has no mooring buoys because an unspoken rule discourages diving in this portion of the reef to allow for safe access by glass-bottom boats. An official "No Anchor Zone" marks the area where, in 1984, the freighter *Wellwood* grounded, pulverizing corals hundreds of years old and flattening the bottom. Over the years, scientists have studied the devastation and worked to rebuild some of the reef structure.

Typical Depth Range:	50 to 130 feet (16-40 m)
Typical Current Conditions:	Strong northerly current (Gulf Stream)
Expertise Required:	Advanced
Access:	Boat

The most dramatic change in Florida Keys diving in recent years has been the addition of a number of ships sunk as artificial reefs. On Thanksgiving weekend in 1987, two of the most spectacular, the U. S. Coast Cutters *Duane* and *Bibb,* were sent to the bottom about one mile offshore of Molasses Reef. The dual sinking culminated a massive community effort to obtain and prepare the 50-year-old vessels for their "final duty" resting on the sea floor awash in the clear waters of the Gulf Stream. Although they are sister ships, they provide two distinct dive sites which are a challenging alternative to diving the shallower natural coral reefs nearby.

The *Duane*. With a slight starboard list, the *Duane* settled upright in 120 feet (37 m) of water facing southwest into the prevailing Gulf Stream current. Descending through clouds of pelagic fish schooled over the wreck, divers can drop down 60 feet below the surface to the crow's nest, which is the highest point of the superstructure, and follow the mast downward. With diver access into the hull blocked off below, the main deck at a depth of 100 feet (32 m) is the best level to begin working a dive. It is seldom advantageous to descend deeper than this.

Forward along the side of the superstructure, rooms and compartments, with doors removed for diver safety, invite exploration. Living creatures have moved in amid the clutter left from shipboard life. Marine growth decorates the surfaces of the vessel softening the outlines of the formerly pristine white bulkheads. A circular hatch in the forward deck marks the ammunition storage area of a former gun turret. A look over the bow to the sandy bottom reveals the anchor chains winding over the relatively featureless terrain that surrounds the ship.

When it is time to ascend, slowly climb the superstructure, deck by deck. Examine the empty wheelhouse and take note of the smoke stack, dented and crumpled from the implosive force of the water rushing inward when she sank. Head back up to the buoy line and remember to make a 10-foot safety stop before surfacing.

One day after sinking, the pristine white superstructure of the Duane *gleams in the clear waters of the Gulf Stream.* ▶

Because the Bibb *lies on her side, the ship's screws are easily accessible. (Photo: J. Halas.)*

The *Bibb*. Four-tenths of a mile to the northeast, the *Bibb* lies on her starboard side in 130 feet (40 m). Although every effort was made to try to get both cutters to land upright on the ocean floor, a trailing starboard anchor probably pulled the *Bibb* over as she sank. As a result, she provides a totally different dive from one on the *Duane*. With the deeper depth, somewhat more risk is involved and the *Bibb* is less often dived.

The broad swell of her hull lies at 90 feet (30 m) with her bow heading northeast in line with the current. Divers must descend and drop over the offshore side to examine the superstructure which extends out across the bottom. The sideways 90° orientation adds another element of challenge to this dive. The interior walls of the structure are beginning to disintegrate and electrical wiring drapes down obscuring the space with spaghetti-like strands. It is best to remain outside and experience the thrill of exploring the *Bibb* exterior.

Both the *Duane* and the *Bibb* are situated where the Gulf Stream current flows strongly. There are times when the current is too great to dive the wrecks safely and divers need to realize that occasionally they might not be able to make a dive.

Once in a while, in this deeper water off the reefline, alert divers may be treated to an experience with larger marine animals. One diver on the *Bibb* looked up to see a giant whale shark nibbling on his bubbles. Big amberjack, huge turtles, and other species of large sharks have been observed from the vessels.

The depth of the Bibb, *her 90° orientation, and a strong current make her suitable for advanced divers only. (Photo: J. Halas.)*

Typical Depth Range:	10-25 feet (3-8 m)
Typical Current Conditions:	Variable but moderate
Expertise Required:	Novice to intermediate
Access:	Boat

Pickles Reef is a versatile diving area located about 2 miles (3 km) southwest of Molasses Reef. The origin of its name is obscure but probably pre-dates what appears to be hardened encrusted pickle barrels scattered around a shipwreck just seaward of the stakes marking the reef. Actually, these small kegs are probably containers of mortar mix or cement that were destined for the great brick forts of Key West and the Dry Tortugas but were lost here.

Like the other outer reefs, Pickles Reef has collected its share of wrecked vessels, both old and new. The remains of a shrimp boat, stranded on the coral crest of the reef, have become a home for many smaller species of fish which are almost immediately attracted to any new habitat suddenly added to the reef environment.

Common on this reef are deep purple sea fans tenaciously anchored to the bottom by the strong grasp of their stems and resolutely facing the wave surge toward the southeast. These lacy fan-like forms are far less delicate than they appear as they sway gently. They are the province of an intriguing photographic subject for close-up or macro photography, the flamingo tongue shell which commonly grazes the sea fan for algae and debris trapped in its filigree network.

Spectacular mollusks, such as the queen conch and the flamingo tongue shell, can be found in profusion at Pickles Reef. Conchs are protected by state law, and no one may take them for any purpose. (Photo: J. Halas.)

A schoolmaster poses in front of a sea fan at Pickles Reef. Sea fans, many with beautiful flamingo tongue shells on them, are common on this reef. (Photo: J. Halas.)

The flamingo tongue, relatively common at Pickles Reef but not always found in similar locations, is about an inch (2.5 cm) long and has an oval flesh-colored shell. Its glory is the magnificent animal within. The mantle, or skin, which emerges and covers the highly polished shell is a transparent yellow with golden leopard spots outlined in black.

Another shell found in the rubble area and grass flats on the back side of Pickles Reef is the queen conch. This is a good area for spotting these large mollusks, which graze here for their food. Although well camouflaged as nondescript rocks, conchs (pronounced "konks" in the Keys) are easy to see once you know what to look for. Look, but do not take, because queen conchs are protected by Florida law and may not be collected for any purpose.

Be sure to visit the "Pillar Coral Forest" on the north end of Pickles Reef. This amazing shallow area has huge pillar coral colonies with fingers stretching 6-10 feet (2-3 m) toward the surface. Storms toppled the top-heavy forms and new fingers, now old, began their upward climb, so that coral grows from coral. While most corals feed at night, this species commonly emerges to eat during the day. Like rusty golden fur, extended coral polyps, living animals encased in limestone "apartments," dance in time to the currents which pass over them. They will disappear at a touch, but take care not to come close enough to brush against these fragile creatures. Touching any corals can abrade them and begin infections which damage and may cause death to the colony.

Typical Depth Range:	Shallow to 100 feet (33 m)
Typical Current Conditions:	Variable, moderate to strong
Expertise Required:	Novice to advanced
Access:	Boat

Conch reef is an extended shallow area that stretches for over a mile (1.5 km) along the outer reef line. Marked with a red nun buoy toward the south end of the main section, many divers enjoy diving Conch Wall, a steep drop just offshore. South of here, an unusual trough 40 feet (13 m) deep cuts in through the reef. All along Conch Reef, exciting diving is commonplace at numerous sites.

On the shallow ledge that runs along the top of the reef north of the buoy, several pillar coral colonies grow in a diagonal line seaward across the ridge. Although some of the colonies are massive, many large pillars are broad, flattened stumps caused by early pruning by coral collectors in the days before all corals were protected.

Offshore of the shallow reefline, the bottom slopes out to 60 feet (19 m) and then drops quite steeply to 90 feet (28 m) or more. These are reminders of an ancient time when lower sea levels cut away the reefline. This 60 to 90 foot drop-off extends all along the Florida Reef tract. "Conch Wall"

Along the rim of the drop-off at Conch Reef, the flow of water promotes the growth of filter-feeding animals, such as this deep-water gorgonian, a soft relative of the coral. (Photo: J. Halas.)

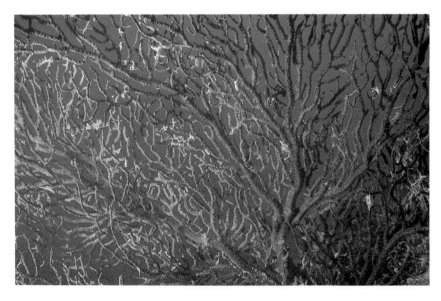

Basket sponges are also common along the drop-off here. The wealth of tiny organisms rushing by in the current causes the sponges to grow to spectacular dimensions. (Photo: J. Halas.)

is a particularly beautiful section of this feature. Along here, the rim does not follow a straight line, but instead "scallops" in and out with the sheerest drops occurring along the promontories or bluffs that project seaward.

On these points, which get the full force of the current, sea life blooms in a variety of forms. Lacy deep-water gorgonians spread out like giant filigree fans along the top of the bluff. Here also, huge purple sponges stand like giant empty vases. Everywhere small deep-water tropicals dart back and forth investigating the bottom growth.

Low-lying star coral colonies glow with unusual coloration. Many of the large polyp star corals are tinted a dusty rose while the small star corals are shaded a delicate turquoise hue. All color in living coral results from algae living in a symbiotic relationship within the coral tissues. Sometimes the corals become stressed, often with rising temperature, and the algae are expelled, resulting in a bleached appearance to the colony.

Dive charters usually anchor along the rim in 60 feet (18 m) where immediately apparent from the surface, sand channels cut through the coral rock like rivulets of sand running down the slope. Divers follow these grooves down to the desired depth and work upcurrent along the base of the reefline. One nice aspect is the ease of relocating the boat since it is hard to miss the anchor line rising from the verge of the steep incline.

Hen and Chickens   12

Typical Depth Range:	20-22 feet (6-7 m)
Typical Current Conditions:	Usually none
Expertise Required:	Novice
Access:	Boat

Hen and Chickens is a rather unusual diving area for an inshore patch reef because of its depth and the size of its corals. Like a bunch of little chicks clustered around a mother hen, this reef is a collection of large star coral heads rising steeply from the bottom and marked by a navigation light. Located close to shore, it provides easy access for small boats and for divers with a limited amount of time who want a good dive.

Overcome by cold Gulf water in 1970, this reef has made a remarkable recovery. New coral growth has appeared and the surfaces of coral structures have been repopulated with soft corals. Now this secondary growth of waving plumes, branching candelabra forms, and broad sea fans adds graceful beauty to the rock contours. Large fish still hide out in hollows beneath the heads, and grouper, grunts, spadefish, sheepshead, porkfish, and snook are commonly seen. Many varieties of angelfish like the inshore areas also.

At Hen and Chickens, the main concentration of coral heads is a bit inshore and north of the light. Remnants of modern wreckage lie just inside the coral clumps on the shoreward edge of the reef. Occasional lobster can be found amid the general debris under the light, and large barracuda patrol here. As with other inshore areas, visibility can vary greatly. Local weather and tide will usually influence the clarity of the water.

Brilliant blue and gold queen angels swim among the coral heads at Hen and Chickens Reef.

The well-named jackknife fish, popular with saltwater aquarium enthusiasts, can be found beneath the ledge at Davis Reef. (Photo: J. Halas.)

Davis Reef 13

Typical Depth Range: Shallow to 80 feet (26 m)
Typical Current Conditions: Variable, little to moderate
Expertise Required: Novice
Access: Boat

Running southwest from the Davis Reef marker is a distinct ledge that makes a fascinating fish-watching dive. Although relatively shallow, Davis Ledge drops off to 25 feet on the inshore side where a wide sand channel borders this old coral ridge. Several large green moray eels live beneath the overhangs in eroded sections of the reef. These creatures, victims of fear propaganda over the years, are actually quite approachable and may become very friendly. Those here at Davis Reef have been pets for years and may slither along with divers, looking for a handout.

Purplish smears in depressions on the bottom are common here. These are the nests of sergeant majors, small yellow and silver fish with black stripes, that will take on a shade of darkish gray when guarding a nest. They aggressively defend their tiny purple eggs from hungry fish determined to nibble on the offspring. Divers should not distract them from this task.

Offshore of Davis Reef, the bottom drops off to 85 feet (26 m) or so, and then rises to a large area of low relief coral ridges and sand channels with a depth of 45 to 50 feet (16 m). Divers who explore this popular fishing area may be rewarded with a surprise find of fishing gear that has been lost overboard.

Typical Depth Range:	75 to 120 feet (23-37 m)
Typical Current Conditions:	Variable, moderate to strong
Expertise Required:	Advanced
Access:	Boat

Lying midway between Crocker Reef and Alligator Light, the *Eagle* is the first of the intact ships deliberately sunk during the 1980s as artificial reefs in the waters off the Upper Keys. Carefully placed charges sent her to the bottom in December, 1985 where she lies now in 120 feet (37 m) of clear Gulf Stream water offshore of the reefline. Originally the *Aaron K,* the 287-foot freighter was renamed the *Eagle* to honor her major sponsor.

The *Eagle* lies on her starboard side with her bow pointed inshore. Her hull is perpendicular to the flow of the northerly Gulf Stream with her superstructure and deck area comfortably in the lee of the often-strong current. Divers can easily explore the ship, sheltered and shielded by the wreck itself.

Follow a buoy line down to the ship's broad hull encountered at a depth of 75 feet (23 m). Divers who drop all the way to the bottom need to watch their depth carefully. The scouring effect of the current can scoop out pockets of sand and the depth can be greater than expected, especially around the giant propellers or the jagged holes blasted in the bottom. Around on the topside of the ship, two large masts extend from

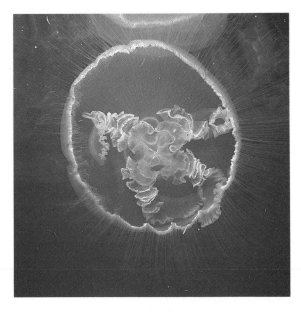

The underside of a moon jellyfish silhouetted against the surface shows its trailing tentacles. Divers surfacing from the Eagle should be alert for these as they ascend. (Photo: J. Halas.)

the forward decks while the ship's smokestacks, bridge, and superstructure are positioned toward the stern.

Prolific fish life surrounds the shipwreck. Stacks of barracuda hang above the vessel, on watch, as schooling fish group themselves in photogenic displays. Amberjacks patrol the perimeter on the lookout for silversides, grunts, and other baitfish. Grouper, cobia, and other common species appear regularly, but spearfishing is not allowed here.

Marine growth covers the *Eagle* and divers should wear protective clothing, especially gloves, on a dive here. The effects of some encrusting hydroids and sponges, unseen or unnoticed, can be powerful. Divers may see clusters of spiny oysters growing on the *Eagle* or other deep wrecks, but they are usually discouraged from collecting these in order to preserve the ecology of the wreck.

A dive on the *Eagle* is an exhilarating experience for advanced divers. As on other deeper dives in the Keys, most shops are very careful to check for proper diving credentials before escorting divers here. Certification cards and logbook documenting recent diving experience are necessities. Divers should check and make arrangements with shops in the area ahead of the time they wish to dive because trips are only scheduled for certain days and during optimum conditions.

The Alexander Barge. Close to the *Eagle* are the remains of other artificial reef structures. One of these is a steel barge where veteran salvage diver, Chet Alexander, lost his life when it went down. Concrete debris from the old Whale Harbor Bridge was also placed here in 110 feet (35 m) of water. The remains rise 12 to 15 feet (3-5 m) from the sand bottom and provide a jumbled habitat for a diverse collection of marine species. Surveys have documented the benefit of these artificial reef structures in increasing the productivity and recruitment in the areas they have been placed.

Clusters of spiny oysters grow on the hulls of many sunken ships, but divers are discouraged from collecting these thorny filter feeders. (Photo: D. Kincaid.)

Typical Depth Range:	12-15 feet (4-5 m)
Typical Current Conditions:	None to moderate
Expertise Required:	Novice
Access:	Boat

In 1733, a fleet of Spanish ships left Havana and were heading northward, laden with New World riches destined for the king of Spain. When they approached Los Martires, now called the Florida Keys, they were driven onto the reefs and into the shallows by a vicious hurricane. The remains of these vessels lay camouflaged by the passing years, until modern technology allowed us to search beneath the sea for its hidden treasures. Innocuous piles of rocks on the ocean floor, ballast stones carried in the lower hold of ships to stabilize them, indicate the location of these ships.

El Infante was such a ship. Nearly an acre of ballast stone, ranging from fist-sized cobbles to huge boulders, was strewn over the shallow bottom marking this treasure wreck with probably the largest ballast pile in the Keys. In the middle of this site, located on Little Conch Reef, are

As with many of the early wooden wrecks in the Keys, a pile of ballast stone is all that remains of the El Infante. *The rocks were carried in the lower hold of ships to lower their center of gravity and keep them stable in heavy seas. (Photo: J. Halas.)*

A scorpionfish rests near the site of the Infante. *These bottom-dwellers look like rocks, sometimes hiding among piles of ballast stone. Spines along their dorsal fins can inject a powerful poison if they are stepped on or brushed. (Photo: J. Halas).*

large timbers protruding from the thickest part of the scattered rocks. These survived, protected from the teredo worms by the sand until recently, and are all that remain of the planking of the ship's deck. Many artifacts have been recovered here, notably the fine, round pillar dollars, beautiful and valuable coins, that were first minted by the Spanish in 1732.

San Pedro, also part of the 1733 fleet, came to rest in the shallow grass bed south of Indian Key. Now, this wreck site is Florida's second Underwater Archaeological Preserve. The ballast pile, one of the earliest artificial reefs, has become the focus of a complex marine ecosystem developed over more than 250 years. The *San Pedro*'s age is accentuated by clusters of coral heads growing on top and cementing the ballast boulders. Seven concrete cannons and a large 18th century ship's anchor have been placed here to enhance the site, which will be reconstructed to appear similar to its original state. Divers and snorkelers should respect the value of this protected historic site and treat it responsibly.

The *Alligator* lies two hundred yards offshore of Alligator Light. Today the U.S.S. *Alligator* is reduced to two large piles of ballast stone fused together with the accretions of nearly two hundred years. In November 1822, the *Alligator* was protecting a convoy from pirates when she grounded on the reef. With the help of a "wrecker" or salvage vessel from the Bahamas, the crew removed everything of value and then set fire to the warship. Shortly afterward, she blew up leaving her mark forever on this reef. Today, visitors to this historic site can reach out and touch history as they explore the shallow wreck. An undercut section of the ballast pile on the south side houses a resident guardian, a watchful moray eel. Perched amid the ballast, scorpion fish lie motionless, looking like just another rock. Divers need to watch out for these toxic fish because a brush with a raised dorsal fin can be extremely painful.

47

4

Diving the Middle Keys

Diving the Middle Keys offers alternatives to the reefs to the north in the Upper Keys. Perhaps the style of the Keys becomes progressively more casual the farther south one travels, but "laid back" is the way things are here. Somehow the sand seems whiter, the water bluer, and the average depth is just a bit shallower on the Middle Keys's reefs allowing for lots of relaxing bottom time.

Traditionally less regulated than other Keys areas, Marathon has been an area where lobstering, fish and shell collecting, and spearfishing activities have been available. Nevertheless, since rules governing these endeavors are continually changing, check with local dive shops for regulations and locations.

Divers in the Middle Keys will appreciate the variety and quantity of fish life in these waters. From tiny tropicals to large food fish, the marine environment is well-populated. Marathon's claim to be "Fishing Capital of the Keys" is deserved.

Dive Site Ratings

Middle Keys	Novice Diver	Novice Diver with Instructor or Divemaster	Intermediate Diver	Intermediate Diver with Instructor or Divemaster	Advanced Diver	Advanced Diver with Instructor or Divemaster
16. Sombrero Reef/ Delta Shoal*	x	x	x	x	x	x
17. Marathon Middle Reefs*	x	x	x	x	x	x
18. The *Thunderbolt*					x	x
19. Content Keys*	x	x	x	x	x	x
20. Looe Key Reef*	x	x	x	x	x	x

* Good snorkeling area

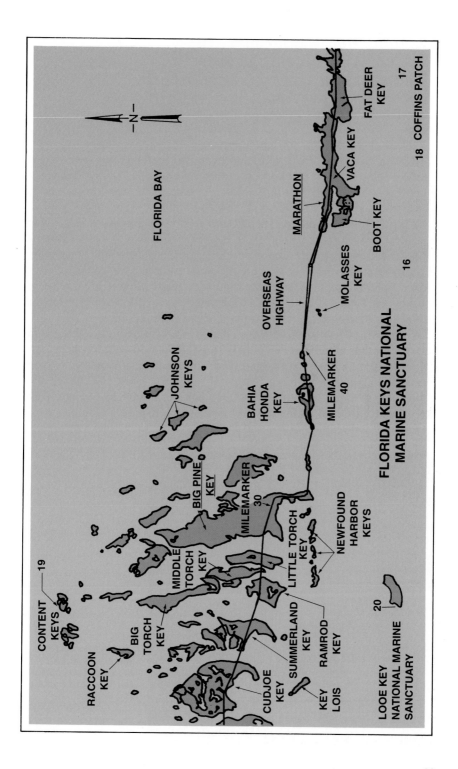

FLORIDA KEYS NATIONAL
MARINE SANCTUARY

Typical Depth Range:	6-25 feet (2-8 m)
Typical Current Conditions:	Variable, light to strong
Expertise Required:	Novice
Access:	Boat

Marked by Sombrero Light, this beautiful reef features well-defined spurs or fingers of reef building corals separated by wide channels of gleaming white sand. Brilliant color and diverse marine life lure divers to this most popular mid-Keys diving site.

A typical dive centers on the central portion of Sombrero Reef where a natural coral bridge about eight feet high forms a feature known as "The Arch." Nearby are mounds of massive star corals. A line of spreading elkhorn stretches back in toward the shallows near the tower. Lots of ledges, overhangs, and hollowed out coral heads provide habitat for sea life and exploring divers. The crooked angles of the reef face lend an interesting backdrop to the schools of fish sheltered there.

At any time, divers might happen upon one of numerous fish cleaning stations in this area. Seeing a fish stopped in mid-water near a coral colony, often with its mouth open, is a sure clue that it is probably being cleaned of minute parasites by tropical reef fish. Look closely for neon gobies, long slivers of blue and black, poking around in and out of the mouth and gills of a cooperative grouper or barracuda.

Brightly colored tube sponges grow on a rounded brain coral. Spots like this become cleaning stations, common at Sombrero Reef, where fish stop by for a check-up. (Photo: J. Halas.)

Most of the colorful reef inhabitants found throughout the Caribbean can be seen at one or another of the Keys dive areas. (Photo: S. Blount.)

Sombrero Reef is dotted with mooring buoys that help protect this remarkable reef system from anchor damage. Working together, the local community raised the necessary funds, and divers contributed time and effort to install the handy buoys. Boaters should use buoys, if available, rather than anchoring.

Delta Shoal. A little more than a mile eastward of Sombrero Light, Delta Shoal is another popular dive site that features massive coral fingers jutting seaward from the shallows. Broad expanses of sandy bottom separate the spurs that form this reef. Convoluted brain corals, flat table rocks, and a series of high relief star coral heads lying off the deeper ends of the reef structure comprise the habitat so attractive to lobster, moray eels, and other tropical reef creatures.

Two interesting wrecks lie in this area. The Delta Shoals Barge is behind the east end. A pretty dive featuring typical shallow water soft corals and an abundance of fish life, this is perfect for snorkeling. The other is the Ivory Coast Wreck, a sunken slave ship lost in 1853 off the west end of Delta Shoal. Little is recognizable any more, but the past yielded many artifacts, even bones, from this wreck site.

Typical Depth Range:	10-25 feet (3-8 m)
Typical Current Conditions:	Light, some tidal current
Expertise Required:	Novice
Access:	Boat

After a deeper dive, like the *Thunderbolt,* dive charter boats will usually head back off the deep reefs for one of the prime shallow dives on Marathon's middle reefs. Any number of locations may be selected depending on the conditions, but a typical choice may be one of the sites on Coffin's Patch. Most are no deeper than 25 feet and all feature an abundance of fish and a variety of coral growth.

At The Donut, divers follow ledges around a roughly circular middle section that rises several feet and is dotted with stony corals and limestone ledges. Larger than normal gray angelfish prowl among rounded convoluted brain corals that measure as much as 6 feet across. Colorful encrusting sponges glowing red, orange, and green, decorate the reef. On the east side, big fleshy anemones hide tiny purple-hued cleaner shrimp that often will emerge to inspect a diver's outstretched hand.

The Stake rises from a rubble zone of eroded, tunneled limestone and fire coral ledges. Actually three more of these reef markers lie underwater, a striking formation that resembles cannons ready to fire. To the west, beautiful large brain corals cluster. Among them, all sizes of trumpetfish hang and glide playing hiding games with divers there.

Photographers will treasure a trip to the Pillar Patch, an area somewhat smaller than a football field filled with huge branching towers of pillar coral. This unusual coral species often has its polyps extended to feed

Abandoned shells quickly become homes for other marine creatures like this hermit crab hiding in a horse conch. Beautiful red sponges lend color to Marathon's inshore reefs. (Photo: J. Halas.)

Underwater, the "Stakes" appear like toppled cannons. This beautiful setting is one of Marathon's popular snorkeling areas. (Photo: J. Halas.)

during the day, so a close look lets people see what the coral animal really looks like. When pillar coral is toppled by storms, it continues to grow at right angles to the fallen branch creating mazes of angular habitat for jewel-like tropicals and invertebrate species common here.

Eastward from Coffin's Patch off Grassy Key, lie a series of ledge systems that are a treat to dive. The Day After, like Yesterday and The Day Before, rises 2-6 feet from an average bottom depth of 25 feet and meanders off to the southeast. At first view, the bottom appears to be alive with motion as an astounding number of predominantly golden fish — grunts, goatfish, and schoolmaster snappers — mill around the area. Sea fans, soft corals, and large sponges top the ledge, which shelters tiny tropicals and crawling bottom dwellers such as hermit crabs, various shells, and lobster.

Unusual pillar coral sends jutting fingers toward the surface. The polyps emerge during the day to feed, giving the colony a fuzzy appearance. (Photo: J. Halas.)

Typical Depth Range: 75-120 feet (22-40 m)
Typical Current Conditions: Moderate to strong
Expertise Required: Advanced
Access: Boat

True to her name, the *Thunderbolt,* a research vessel once used for studying lightning, has become a "striking" dive site! The 188-foot ship rests upright in 120 feet of water offshore of the east end of Marathon, sunk there in March, 1986.

A dive to the *Thunderbolt* begins by descending the permanent buoy line down through clouds of silvery baitfish, drifting barracuda, and circling amberjack. At 85 feet, her bow is dominated by a huge horizontal reel, a reminder of her early use as a cable layer during World War II. The rim and spokes of this giant cable spool are softened and fringed with marine organisms. Heading back amidships, the dive will probably center on the broad bridge that rises to 80 feet. An opening in the base of the superstructure gives inside access to a stairway that rises to the wheelhouse at the top. Ascending to this level, divers will usually encounter a solitary barracuda standing watch at the helm. Swimming through the compartments and around the exterior passageways gives a sailor's eye view of the underwater scene. Continuing back along the main deck, large hatches open into the engine compartments where it is possible to descend into the hull to 110 feet. Dropping back over the stern of the vessel, divers can examine the huge twin props that once powered this proud ship.

The cable spool on the bow of the Thunderbolt *provides a unique photo opportunity, but divers and models need to be well-protected and cautious of stinging hydroids and sponge growth. (Photo: J. Halas.)*

Two crustacean delicacies are found in abundance near the Content Keys, lobsters and stone crabs. Though both are easy pickings for divers, check the game regulations before stuffing any in your game bag. (Photo: D. Kincaid.)

Content Keys   19

Typical Depth Range:	8-15 feet (1-4.5 m)
Typical Current Conditions:	Minimal
Expertise Required:	Novice
Access:	Boat

The Content Keys, uniquely positioned on the Gulf side southwest of Marathon, are sheltered by the Keys and lie in the lee of prevailing winds. This dive site, though shallow and lacking "crystal" visibility, is a good calm alternative on windy days.

The Gulf side of the Keys supports an entirely different ecosystem from the ocean side. Occasionally, corals that tolerate greater changes in temperature and lower light levels, like the rounded starlet corals, grow here. Dives usually begin at the Content Ledges just offshore of the Keys. This rocky shelf extends east and west and rises 2 or 3 feet (1 m) from the 10-foot (3-m) sea bottom. Numerous potholes and cracks in the coral rock make and ideal habitat for both lobster and stone crab. Even the locals come to this area for these delicacies.

Offshore, a 10-minute boat ride away, a collection of large coral heads, rare on the Gulf side, rise from a depth of 12 feet (4 m). Here divers can spread out and wander among these massive living boulders.

Typical Depth Range:	5-35 feet (2-11 m)
Typical Current Conditions:	Light to moderate
Expertise Required:	Novice to intermediate and advanced
Access:	Boat

About 7 miles (11 km) south of Ramrod Key lies one of the loveliest, most varied and prolific reefs in the Florida Keys, Looe Key.

In 1744, Captain Ashby Utting accidently ran his frigate, the H.M.S. *Looe,* hard aground, thus giving the key its name. The remains of the ship lie between two fingers of coral near the eastern end of the reef about 200 yards (155 m) from the marker. Although the ballast and a heavily encrusted anchor remain, only the trained eye can distinguish them from the reef. Because all of Looe Key is now designated a marine sanctuary, no spear fishing, lobstering, or artifact recovery is permitted. "Look but don't touch."

Looe Key is a geological anomaly. It is totally unlike any of the reefs of the Lower Keys in structure or in variety of life. Looe Reef contains

Looe Key, a national marine sanctuary, is a perfect example of a spur-and-groove reef system. Long fingers of coral fan out over a white sand bottom, which forms gullies between the rows of coral heads. (Photo: D. Kincaid.)

Coral polyps and featherworms form a modern-art mosaic at Looe Key, named for the H.M.S. Looe, a British ship that sank here. (Photo: D. Kincaid.)

species of coral found in both the patch reefs and outside reefs as opposed to other sites farther west that only contain fingers of fire coral, elkhorn and staghorn coral.

Looe also has large quantities of sand at its base, which spill out slowly in a never-ending cascade southward into the ocean abyss nearby, and is washed constantly by the waters of the Gulf Stream. Looe Key's pulsating life cycle is continually renewed by larval creatures that drop from the sargasso weed and propagate the reef. Although parts of the reef are awash, the fingers of coral base have gullies approaching 35 feet (11 m) deep in some spots, topped by monastera and waving sea fans. This unique structure, blue water, and moderate current combine to make an idyllic dive.

Marine Life. Temperatures year round seldom require more than a wet suit top. Fishes from several different environmental zones congregate here burrowing yellow-headed jawfish, parrots, and surgeonfish on the north side behind the reef rubble. Barracudas and jacks on top of the reef, grunts, cotton wicks and angels on the reef proper, and rays, lizardfish and an occasional peacock flounder on the sandy floor on seaward side. Several commercial dive boats visit Looe Key; most leave from Big Pine Key.

The reef is roughly 200 yards (155 m) wide and 800 yards (750 m) long and is roughly Y-shaped. In short, Looe Key is a rewarding and exciting dive for all levels of expertise and is probably the most beautiful reef in the lower keys.

5

Diving the Lower Keys

Divers from the frozen north who drive into the Lower Keys enter a wonderland of wet delights. As the only highway leaps from bridge to bridge, just a short swim or boat ride away are reefs, shallows, islands, and currents unparalleled in the diversity of their wildlife. This area has been described as "a land that's mostly water and a sea that's mostly sky."

Dive Site Ratings

Lower Keys	Novice Diver	Novice Diver with Instructor or Divemaster	Intermediate Diver	Intermediate Diver with Instructor or Divemaster	Advanced Diver	Advanced Diver with Instructor or Divemaster
21. South Beach Patches and	x	x	x	x	x	x
Key West Harbor				x	x	x
22. Sand Key	x	x	x	x	x	x
23. Outside Reefs			x	x	x	x
24. Rock Key and						
Eastern Dry Rocks	x	x	x	x	x	x
25. Western Dry Rocks						
(The K Marker)	x	x	x	x	x	x
26. Chef's Wreck #1	x	x	x	x	x	x
27. Joe's Tug			x	x	x	x
28. Cottrell Reef						
(Gulf Side Reef)*	x	x	x	x	x	x
29. The Lakes*	x	x	x	x	x	x
30. Marquesas Keys	x	x	x	x	x	x
31. The Wrecks in Marquesas	x	x	x	x	x	x
32. Cosgrove Shoal			x	x	x	x
33. Marquesas Rock			x	x	x	x

* Good snorkeling area

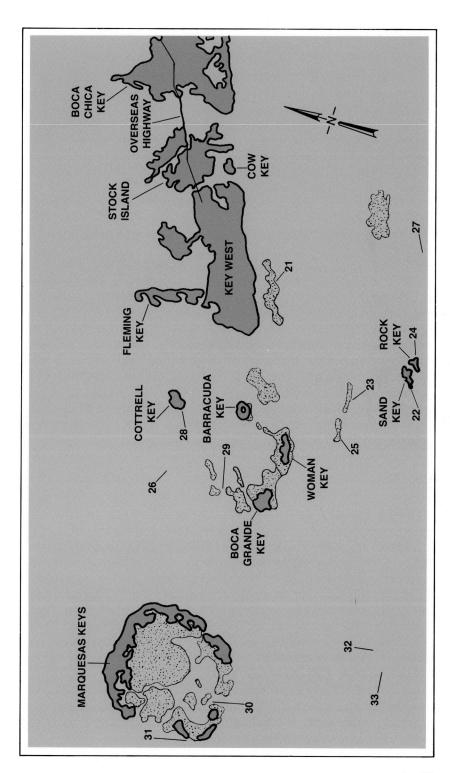

Geology. The Keys island chain runs roughly east and west, not north and south as many people assume. On the north or Gulf of Mexico side are dozens of mangrove islands and wading birds. On the south or Atlantic side are the reefs, washed by the Gulf Stream that great river in the sea that meanders up the east coast of the United States.

The Lower Keys contain several basic geological and environmental zones. Southernmost are the Outside and Barrier reefs, with fishes and coral influenced by the Caribbean and Gulf Stream; immediately to the north, between the reefs and the Keys, Hawk Channel has a generally muddy or sandy bottom and intermittent patch reefs that rise very near the surface in some areas. Farther north are the Keys proper, or back country, a mangrove nursery area for most of Florida's commercial fisheries and essentially an estuarine environment similar to and influenced by the shallows of Florida Bay, the Everglades, and the Gulf of Mexico, which is a large, relatively shallow partially enclosed sea. Because of this mix of marine influences, the Keys generally have a wider variety of fish and coral than even some areas of the Caribbean. The transitional area between the Keys and the Gulf is a hard rocky ledge that runs from the Content Keys north of Big Pine and southwest past Cottrell Key. This ledge is similar to what is called "ironshore" throughout the Caribbean, a sort of compact conglomerate of shells, coral, and fine sand fused together by thousands of years of pressure. Occasionally, this rocky substrate will be cratered like Swiss cheese, where pockets of organic material have rotted and formed an acidic solution that eats huge holes called solution holes. Many of these holes are aggravated and enlarged by wave action.

Unique Diving Services. Most of the dive shops in the Keys offer some type of charter dive service, but there are several that are unique.

Earl DeTurk of Big Pine Key offers custom dive trips aboard his 41-foot (12 m) Chinese junk-rigged trimaran *Water Spyder*. Earl is a naturalist and consequently looks at the Keys through different eyes from most of us. He not only day-sails *Water Spyder* but will do week-long excursions on request. If you hate sailing on conventional keel boats, *Water Spyder* is a treat because it sails flat and doesn't roll at all. You can actually set your drink down in a civilized manner without it sliding out of reach and falling onto the deck. Earl does not do scuba trips, only free diving from this unique craft. Earl works out of the Looe Key Reef Resort.

Another special trip is given by Captain Vicki Impalomeni. This vivacious lady is also a marine biologist and avid environmentalist who specializes in family trips. While Mom and Dad dive, Captain Vicki will teach the little ones about the wonders of the Keys.

Lost Reef Adventures in Land's End Village is one of only three full service dive shops in Key West. Family-owned and operated with the widest range of specialty boats available, it is highly recommended for all watersports activities.

Tom Jackson of Sea and Sail Excursions also runs special trips, primarily video safaris to the Marquesas Keys. These all-day excursions are a must. When you visit the Marquesas with Tom, chances are you will have the whole place to yourself because few divers visit this exotic locale.

Recently, several large sailing catamarans have started operations in Key West. They all do snorkeling trips to the reefs, but the new pride of the fleet is Dennis Conner's *Stars and Stripes, Key West*. Named by Dennis after his America's Cup winning boats, this special vessel was designed and built especially for the waters of the Lower Keys. *Stars and Stripes* sports a two foot draft, glass bottom windows, a fully shaded lounge, and she daily visits the out-island beaches and many hidden reefs few tourists ever see.

One other special trip that should be noted is run by Captain Billy Deans of Deans of Key West Divers on Stock Island. Billy specializes in shipwrecks. His premier dive probably is the *Wilkes Barre*, a World War II ship sunk in 145-250 feet (45-77 m) of water in the Gulf Stream. Billy's boat, the *Key West Diver*, is specially set up for deep diving with oxygen decompression hookah gear.

A diver examines an unusual coral formation at Sand Key in the Lower Keys. (Photo: D. Kincaid.)

Typical Depth Range:	15 feet (5 m) reefs/30feet (10 m) harbor
Typical Current Conditions:	Light on reefs but strong on harbor
Expertise Required:	Novice/intermediate on reefs, advanced in harbor
Access:	Beach or boat

All along the southern shore of Key West (and in fact all the Lower Keys), from 150-400 yards out, are scores of coral patches and reefs. Some are just individual heads, but others are extensive sets that cover many acres of ocean floor. The most prominent ones are off the foot of Duval Street, Simonton Street, immediately off of the Casa Marina Hotel, at the end of Bertha Street, off the main bathing beach, and off the airport. Probably the easiest ones to find are off the dock at the Casa Marina Hotel, where several markers can be seen. These mark a channel through the coral heads. Directly east and west of these marks are coral patches

The South Beach Patches near Key West hold innumerable fascinating creatures such as this basket starfish. (Photo. D. Kincaid.)

◀ *The graceful flamingo tongue shell can often be found grazing on sea fans. The beautiful golden spots are not on the shell, but are actually the mantle of the mollusk inside. (Photo: D. Kincaid.)*

A spotted moray wedges itself into a crevice beneath a variety of sponges on the South Beach Patches. (Photo: D. Kincaid.)

covering several acres of sea floor. Snappers and grunts are common as well as groupers and an occasional jewfish. In the grassy flats nearby are many eating-size conches and, of course, lobsters in the mud ledges and under coral heads. Almost any fish life that you might normally find on the outside reef can be found here. There is seldom much current, and visibility is generally 15-40 feet (5-12 m), with the average about 30 feet (10 m). All patch reefs along the Keys are in 12-15 feet (4-5 m) of water and are found near shallow ledges or changes in depth. It has been speculated that they are probably the remains of Florida's ancient shore line. Although these areas are an easy swim from shore, you should always have a float or inner tube with a diving flag prominently displayed, because on weekends and near the end of the day there can be a lot of boat traffic in these areas.

Advanced Divers. At the north end of Simonton Street is a small public boat ramp and dingy landing area that gives access to Key West Harbor. This harbor has been in use since the middle of the 16th century, and consequently the bottom is loaded with old bottles and artifacts as well as lobsters and grouper. Even though you have beach access here, a tank should be used in the 20-30 feet (6-10 m) depths because of heavy commercial boat traffic. Visibility is about 15 feet (5 m) with an extremely heavy current. This area is for *advanced divers only*. One favorite trick is to check where the cruise ships have been after they have left, because their prop wash can stir up the bottom, revealing the goodies. If you have a boat, a drift dive may turn up Spanish olive jars or bottles from the 19th century.

Typical Depth Range:	Awash to 30-65 feet (10-20 m)
Typical Current Conditions:	Light to moderate
Expertise Required:	All levels
Access:	Boat

Sand Key was originally called Cayos Arena by the early Spanish explorers of the Keys. It is a simple sand island without vegetation, topped by a red iron lighthouse that was built in 1853 and is now on the historical register. According to the Spaniards, the island was "changeable according to the rigors of the weather." Indeed, with every winter storm or summer hurricane the shape of Sand Key changes. Upon close examination, the island turns out to be less sand than ground-up coral and small shells. Anyone wanting a collection of miniature shells can certainly find them here.

Because it can be seen for miles, the Sand Key Lighthouse is easy to find and is probably the most popular dive spot in the Lower Keys. It is not unusual to see several dozen divers and a hundred snorkelers here at a time. Yet, there is never really a crowd because of the size and diversity of the reef and lagoon areas.

Through the efforts of Reef Relief, a local environmental organization, the Key West community has worked together to install mooring buoys

The lighthouse and beautiful shallow reef formations of Sand Key are clearly visible from the air. Recently, a serious fire damaged the historic light. (Photo: D. Kincaid.)

at Sand Key and other popular dive sites. These buoys prevent anchor damage to the corals and other marine life and should be used when available rather than anchoring.

The reef itself is typical of major Lower Keys reefs, consisting mostly of rock fingers and gullies of 5-20 feet (2-6 m) deep, with sandy bottoms between cliff-like structures. Several sections of the reef have rather extensive areas of staghorn and elkhorn coral, and fire coral abounds. The northwest side of the reef has numerous coral heads and mixed rubble in close proximity to the lagoon and is more suitable to beginners. The south side of the reef gradually slopes away to a gentle ledge at about 65 feet (20 m), dropping to 90 feet (28 m) in some places. Also in the shallows are artifacts from the brick lighthouse, which blew away in 1846. Visibility at Sand Key can be highly variable depending on the wind, wave action, and monthly tide variations. At its worst it can be about 15 feet (5 m) and at its best over 100 feet (30 m), but the average is 30-60 feet (10-20 m). Spring and summer are the best times to visit Sand Key because the nearby Gulf Stream blows in over the shallows, adding an extra sparkle to the saturated oranges and yellows that dominate the reef structure.

A paradise for divers and snorkelers, Sand Key offers stands of elkhorn coral in very shallow water. (Photo: D. Kincaid.)

Typical Depth Range:	40-210 feet (12-63 m)
Typical Current Conditions:	Moderate
Expertise Required:	Intermediate and advanced
Access:	Boat

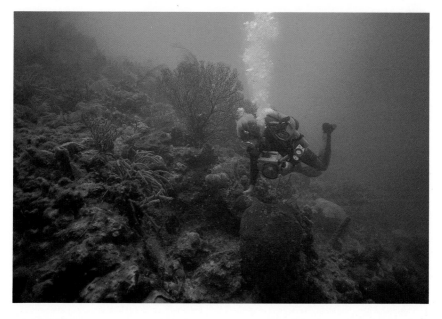

The ledge of the drop-off along the Outside Reefs is typical of Caribbean formations, offering large heads of brain and star corals, along with deep-water gorgonians. (Photo: D. Kincaid.)

For the more experienced diver, a dive on the outside reefs is a must. All along the Keys, just south of the main shallow reefs, are the Gulf Stream reefs. These are the last diveable reefs in America before you get to the open sea. Also known as the Outside Bar, the Hump, 10 Fathom Bar, or Eyeglass Bottom, they are usually about a half-mile to a mile (1 to 1½ km) into the Stream off the main reefs. Because they are all similar, we will only discuss one here; the rest are all on standard nautical charts. A few minutes' run south from Sand Key, the water starts to shallow up again, reaching about 40 feet (12 m) at its shallowest, with a white sandy bottom. Eighty percent of the time the visibility is 80-100 feet (25-30 m) so you can just look over the side or use your fathometer; but when you get to 65 feet (19 m), that's the drop-off and the last place you can anchor easily. The area above the drop-off is a lush prolific gallery of rarely seen deep-water corals and fish, reminiscent of deep walls in the Caymans and Bahamas. Over the drop-off the light is dimmer and there is not as

A nudibranch clambers over encrusted coral rock along the Outside Reefs. The animals are also called sea slugs, and come in various bright colors. (Photo: D. Kincaid.)

much growth. The base of the reef varies from 110 to 210 feet (33-63 m) where a gradual slope of rubble leads toward the ocean abyss.

One of my (Kincaid's) favorite sightings was a 500-member school of giant tarpon that ranged from 7 to 12 feet (2-3 m) in length. (I have witnesses!) Because the full life cycle of the tarpon isn't known, this school of record-breakers was phenomenal.

Probably the best way to dive here is to start in the deep water and work your way up to the 40-foot (12-m) level as partial decompression, then move back to Sand Key for another dive. There are several places along the wall where encrusted telephone cables spin off into the blue mist to Cuba, sponges are big enough to stand in, and black coral is shrouded with carousing Lilliputian life forms.

The current is occasionally strong but usually moderate, and water temperature even in winter is usually above 75°F (24°C) thanks to the Gulf Stream. The deep reefs are different from anything anywhere else in the Keys. When you dive there and look to the deep sea, you are on the last bit of ground in America and have the entire rest of the U.S.A. at your back.

Typical Depth Range:	5-35 feet (2-11 m)
Typical Current Conditions:	Light
Expertise Required:	All levels
Access:	Boat

Rock Key and Eastern Dry Rocks are just east of Sand Key Light, about a mile (1½ km) and 1½ miles (2½ km), respectively. Both are typical of most reef formations in the area, with a rubble zone on top and long fingers of coral with sand and coral-filled canyons in between. Both are very popular dive spots with lots of shells, conches, lobsters, and fish, but their real claim to fame, besides their lush beauty, are the wrecks that are here.

Each reef is topped with rusted poles and both usually have breakers in all but the calmest weather. Depending on the wind, the best anchorages are usually on the western ends where there is generally less swell and a sandy bottom, because the battle between anchors and coral is usually lost by the coral.

On top of Rock Key, in about 6 feet (2 m) of water, are a number of large cement beams. In this area just beneath the sand lies a huge quantity of pebble ballast; because few people collected rocks in the 18th and 19th centuries, this area is a Mecca for lapidary workers. Many of the rocks are quartz and there are several types of volcanic stone that can be polished to perfection and made into belt buckles, pendants, and so on. There are also a lot of tiles that say "Barcelona," brass spikes, and cannon balls.

On the western end of Eastern Dry Rocks in the second finger gully, just before the water is shallow enough for a person to stand up, is the remains of another 19th century wreck site. With ballast stones covering the bottom for over 100 yards (90 m), anyone with patience or a metal detector can just fan away with a ping pong paddle and be rewarded with brass spikes, cannon balls, or an occasional bit of rigging. Because the average wreck yields over 250,000 artifacts, you can fan around for a long time, have a lot of fun, and never make a dent in the site. Most of the dive boats from Key West stop at these two reefs, so if in doubt just ask the captain for directions.

Much of the Key's underwater beauty is accessible to the snorkeler. (Photo: D. Kincaid.)

Typical Depth Range:	5-120 (2-36 m)
Typical Current Conditions:	Light to moderate
Expertise Required:	Novice to advanced
Access:	Boat

Just west of Sand Key, about 3 miles (5 km), is a fine reef called Western Dry Rocks or the K Marker. The K Marker is not dived as often as Sand Key or other popular reefs closer to Key West, and consequently has not suffered the inevitable anchor damage that other reefs have. It is just a little farther away than most weekend divers like to go, but is well worth the trip. Unless there has been severe weather recently, K Marker usually has clearer visibility than Sand Key, Rock Key, or Eastern Dry Rocks; reefs that straddle the major natural and shipping channels out of Key West.

Marine Life. The formation of Western Dry Rocks is typical of most of the Lower Key structure reefs: long fingers of cliff-like corals with sandy gullies in between. The K Marker has more cracks and crevices and many more caves than any other reef here. Species normally found in the Bahamas or on the deep outer reefs may be found, primarily candy basslets, orange back bass, and an occasional pygmy angelfish or long snout butterflyfish. This reef is also the last of the reefs to the west with water shallow enough to have elkhorn and staghorn coral in any quantity before the Tortugas. The best anchorage is on the large sand bars at the western or northwestern end of the reef, or behind the reef rubble zone

The Western Dry Rocks offers a series of coral undercuts and ledges in water shallow enough for snorkelers. (Photo: D. Kincaid.)

Large marine life, such as this sea turtle can be found hiding in the caves at the Western Dry Rocks. (Photo: D. Kincaid.)

on the north side. The rubble zone can be waded at low tide, but is definitely not for non-swimmers. There are several large stands of coral on top of the reef and much debris from former reef markers and wrecks. These chunks of debris usually have lobsters. At certain times of the year, as many as 30 sharks can be seen patrolling the top of the reef. This is evidently part of their mating ritual. If you see them, stay in the deeper water near your boat and *don't* spear fish or catch lobster; sharks will definitely come to the dinner bell and at these times they don't have good manners. Usually they are black tips and bull or lemon sharks, but an occasional oceanic hammerhead might be seen.

In several of the coral gullies of this reef you may find wreck material including lead sheathing, spikes, nails, and ballast. Many ships have struck this reef during the last couple of centuries. One crack in the reef even contains ballast stones embedded 8½ feet (3 m) under solid coral. At a growth rate of ¼ inch (6 mm) a year, that makes this wreck 400 years old. Most debris here is about middle to late 19th century.

Large jacks and permit can also be seen, usually in the spring and early summer. Water depths range from 15-25 feet (5-8 m), but there is a gradual slope to 120 feet (36 m) with sponges, coral, sea fans, and huge grouper. Water temperatures are just a little cooler here, but at the coldest only about 70° F (21° C). Visibility can be exceptional. I (Kincaid) once anchored in what I thought was about 60 feet (18 m) of water and my anchor took out 150 feet (45 m) of line before it touched bottom.

Typical Depth Range: Awash to 30 feet (10 m)
Typical Current Conditions: Moderate to strong
Expertise Required: Novice to intermediate and advanced
Access: Boat

Local commercial salvor Chet Alexander has probably sunk more ships in and around the Lower Keys than any other individual — a destroyer escort, several barges, and a tug boat, to mention a few. His most popular dive site is a destroyer escort, locally known as Alexander's Wreck, that Chet bought from the Navy for $2,000 and moved to this isolated location.

Although popular, the wreck is only occasionally visited by commercial dive boats. If you want to dive there commercially, you must ask. The wreck lies due west 5 miles (8 km) off the #4 buoy near the Gulf entrance to the Northwest channel and about 3 miles (5 km) north northwest of Little Mullet Key in about 25-30 feet (8-10 m) of water. Alexander's Wreck is broken in half, with the stern section lying 150 yards (135 m) or so north of the bow, which is awash on most tides. Despite the fact that part of the hull is clear of the water, the wreck is difficult to see. A number of captains have hit the jagged metal tear that juts above the water, ruining props and rudders.

A diver closes in for a macrophotograph on the crumpled steel hull of Chet's Wreck. (Photo: D. Kincaid.)

A pair of spadefish hover over the sand near Chet's Wreck #I. (Photo: D. Kincaid.)

Marine Life. This former naval vessel lies on its side and is home for thousands of fish. At different times of the year, different fish life can he found. Sheepshead, spadefish, porkfish, groupers, hogfish, snappers and angels are thick, with an occasional mackerel or jewfish making a visit. Spearfishers love this wreck. The hull itself is covered with leafy oysters and jewel boxes, and occasionally cowries or spiny oysters can be found in the gun turrets.

Visibility is not quite as good on the Gulf side of the Keys as on the reef, but this area will usually average about 25-40 feet (8-12 m). In the winter, water temperatures will be 69-74° F (20-23° C), but even in the summer when the water temperature is in the 80s (about 28-32° C) a wet suit and gloves should be worn, simply because of the jagged metal on the wreck and the stinging hydroids that cover the hulls.

At times the current can he very strong in this area, but generally not more than most divers can handle. Even novices can take great delight in snorkeling over the 2 parts of the site because the wreckage is generally visible from the surface. It is usually best to anchor away from the site and trail a safety line with a float on the end for returning to your vessel. The bottom in this area is covered with gorgonians and sponges. Always send the first diver in the water to check the anchor's set because of the hard and relatively flat bottom.

Typical Depth Range:	65 feet (21 m)
Typical Current Conditions:	Light to moderate
Expertise Required:	Intermediate to advanced
Access:	Boat

Recently, a small tugboat was discovered sitting serenely on the bottom in 65 feet (21 m) of water on the outer slope of the reef. Called Joe's Tug after Joe Weatherby, the diver who found it, this small vessel was obviously stripped and dumped, or else it drifted to this location.

The boat sits upright and is an easy swim through. Photographers will find this is an excellent location with cooperative subjects and good panoramic views. The wheel house and aft deck have open access and divers will enjoy poking around.

Because the tug is situated on the outside reef, visibility is usually quite good, often over 60 feet and occasionally over 100 feet. Clouds of fish surround the wreck. Its deck is at a depth of 40 feet (13 m) and many small tropicals have made their homes here. The bottom around the tug hosts a wide variety of coral colonies and varied deep reef marine life.

This is a simple dive for beginning divers with open-water experience, but it is still a enjoyable adventure for the more advanced or photo-oriented visitor.

She may be small in size, but Joe's Tug presents an eerie sight underwater. (Photo: ▶
D. Kincaid.)

Sunken ships, such as Joe's Tug, provide opportunities for unusual photographs, such as this "diver in a basket." (Photo: D. Kincaid.)

Typical Depth Range:	3-15 feet (1-5 m)
Typical Current Conditions:	Light to moderate
Expertise Required:	Novice or intermediate
Access:	Boat

Cottrell Reef is considered by most local divers to be an alternative dive spot when the weather blows up on the Atlantic side of the Keys. It is a shallow (3-15 feet or 1-5 m deep) rocky ledge, protected from strong east southeast and southwest winds by miles of grassy banks called the Lakes. The ledges and banks of Cottrell start just west of the old house on stilts at the Gulf entrance to the North West channel. These ledges and solution holes are covered with gorgonians and sponges, and run for a couple of miles before finally disappearing beneath the sands.

A photographer examines the cobbled surface of a coral head near Cottrell Reef. (Photo: D. Kincaid.)

A *Lima* clam and a convict
goby enliven this batch of
encrusting orange
sponge on Cottrell Reef.
(Photo: D. Kincaid.)

Marine Life. Intermittently along the ledge are large clusters of coral heads. The top part of the reef is flat and ideal for waders, but just a dozen feet (4 m) away are pits, crevices, and coral caves carved by wave action. The bottoms of most solution pits are natural catch basins for shells. Weaving about these convolutions are a wide variety of juvenile reef fish, as well as many adults, mostly parrots and snappers.

According to Betty Bruce, historian at the Key West library, Cottrell Key was named after the Captain of the lightship that was anchored nearby in the early 19th century. The visibility at Cottrell is generally l5-40 feet (5-12 m), and even on rough days there is seldom much current or surge. Consequently, Cottrell is an excellent reef for beginning snorkelers. All of the commercial operations in Key West make this reef part of their itinerary when the weather is bad on the main reef.

Typical Depth Range:	5-30 feet (2-10 m)
Typical Current Conditions:	Light, except in channels where it can be quite strong
Expertise Required:	All levels
Access:	Boat

Directly west of Key West is a fascinating and varied snorkeling area known as the Lakes. A series of grassy flats and banks completely encompass a shallow lagoon that starts at Mule Key and runs west 9 miles (14 km) to Boca Grand Key. This shallow area is seldom more than 10 feet (3 m) deep, and is usually less than 6 feet (2 m). It is completely protected from wave action by the flats, and usually has reasonably clear water even in the worst winds. The area boasts several modern wrecks, coral and lobster-filled channels, coral heads, sponge bars loaded with groupers and snappers, and islands with white sandy beaches. Large expanses of the Lakes are shallow and impassable, so if you go in your own boat, it is best to use a local guide or perhaps acquire topographic maps of the area, because regular nautical charts are only of moderate assistance here.

The best known diving spots in the area are two target ships just north of Boca Grand Key. A large, deep channel on the west side of the island leads right up to the wrecks, one of which sticks out of the water and can be seen for miles. The other is submerged about 100 yards (90 m) south in a finger channel. Both wrecks are covered with edible oysters

The Lakes are a series of shallow lagoons protected by a string of islands and reefs. (Photo: D. Kincaid.)

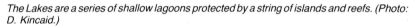

Nudibranchs, which means "naked gills," are so called because their gills are exposed. The graceful ruffles along this nudibranch's back are its breathing organs. (Photo: D. Kincaid.)

and clouds of snappers, grunts, and an occasional school of snook (don't shoot, it's against the law), as well as an abundance of sea urchins.

The current on an outgoing tide can be much too strong for most people to swim against. Tide charts and good timing are a must, of course. If you wish to dive any of the channels in the Lakes at just any time, make it a drift dive, which covers more territory anyway.

Several islands in the Lakes have the letters *m u l e* in their names. This is left over from the ancient Spanish name for the islands, *Chici Mulei* (little brothers). These are some of the oldest place names still in use in the United States, dating back to the early 16th century. There are over 2 dozen major channels in the Lakes and some 40 sponge bars, with dozens of coral heads — far too many to explain here. With a good pair of polarized sunglasses, a couple of charts, and a shallow-draft boat, the astute diver should have no trouble exploring these fascinating mangrove islands. Don't forget to look beneath the mangrove roots; under these islands is a hanging garden of marine life, unparalleled in its diversity, with numerous colored sponges and "macrolife." It is also a nursery area for almost all of Florida's commercial species.

Typical Depth Range:	5-30 feet
Typical Current Conditions:	Light on coral heads; moderate to strong in channels
Expertise Required:	All levels
Access:	Boat

The Marquesas Keys are the only known atoll in the Atlantic Ocean. Unlike their Pacific counterparts, which are volcanic in origin, these skull shaped islands are quite possibly the remains of a prehistoric meteor crater. The islands were named in 1623 for the Marquis de Cadereita, commander of the ill-fated 1622 Spanish treasure fleet, which included the famous wrecks of the *Atocha* and *Santa Margarita*.

The circle of islands is about 3½ miles (5½ km) across and 22 miles (32 km) west of Key West, or about an hour's run by outboard, and like most of the Lower Keys is a bird sanctuary and National Wilderness Area. The Markeys, as they are called by locals, contain the only frigate bird rookery in the United States, and several of the islands have long, white, sandy beaches where pottery dating from 1622 can be found. There are also excellent anchorages in the various creeks between the islands. However, much of the lagoon is shallow and relatively impassable. There

A crinoid, or feather starfish, ducks into a small hole in the reef of the Marquesas Key. (Photo: D. Kincaid.)

Delicate Christmas tree worms cover the surface of this coral head. (Photo: D. Kincaid.)

are several wrecks in the area all of which are accurately placed on nautical charts. Huge clusters of coral heads can be found about 300 yards (270 m) off the entire southern edge of the islands in about 8-12 feet (3-4 m) of water. Some of these are shallow enough to hit with your prop, but are also marked on the charts. The wrecks in this area are famous for jewfish, permit, and cobia, but the coral heads are most noted for grouper, snapper, and lobster. Although the Markeys are a good run from Key West, if you have the time and the gas they are worth it. They are only visited by serious divers and anglers; the islands show little evidence of man and probably look very much as they did in 1622.

Although it's only about 5½ miles (8 km) from the protected Lakes area, the crossing of Boca Grande Channel can be quite rough if the wind and tide are in opposition. Be sure to select your weather, spare parts, and radio with care and all the considerations of good seamanship.

Typical Depth Range: 15-20 feet (5-6 m)
Typical Current Conditions: Moderate to strong
Expertise Required: All levels
Access: Boat

West of the Marquesas lie several wrecks of interest to divers. The first is a little more than a half mile (1 km) west of the westernmost cut of the Markeys, sometimes called Houseboat Cut because of the Treasure Salvors house boat that was anchored in the cut for a couple of years. This wreck was a target ship for the Navy many years ago and lies in a north-south position astride the first major sand bar off the cut. Parts of the wreck are shallow and just below the surface, so don't break your propeller here; it's a long way to the nearest repair shop. Large chunks of jagged metal lie in a ship-shaped pile, along with many old bomb casings. The sand bar shifts constantly; at times the wreck is completely covered, at other times well exposed.

About 3½ miles (5½ km) farther west lies another target vessel, a destroyer escort called the *Patricia* target ship. The wreck is easy to find because it is surrounded by a dozen large I-beams that stick out of the water about 15 feet (5 m). This ship is still actively bombed by the Navy and Marines, so if a military jet makes a low pass over the ship, that's your signal to leave the area because firing will commence shortly and you must move off at least a mile (1½ km) or two. Anchor and have a snack because the show can be spectacular.

The jewfish is gigantic member of the grouper family. Generally, they are a minimum of 4 feet (1 m) long when fully grown, and jewfish up to 6 feet (2 m) long and weighing 600 pounds are not uncommon. (Photo: D. Kincaid.)

Some of the wrecks in the Marquesas are shallow enough for snorkelers to enjoy as well. (Photo: D. Kincaid.)

Fish Among the Wreck. The *Patricia* is about 150 feet (45 m) long and is now reduced to piles of jagged metal. Most of the rockets that are fired are practice bombs containing little more than shotgun shells, so they seldom do much damage and the fish life is unaffected. Although the current can be severe, it is usually easy to get behind a large chunk of the ship to calmer water. You should always wear gloves and some body protection when diving these wrecks because of the jagged metal and stinging hydroids. It is not recommended to attempt any penetration of the *Patricia*; it is an extremely unstable wreck because of the bombing. Its configuration changes constantly, with large sections collapsing all the time.

If all this shooting business sounds like an outrageous way to go diving, take heart. The *Patricia* is seldom bombed more than a couple of days out of the month and is only usually worked over every three months or so. Bombing times and dates are listed in the newspapers and are on the radio. If in doubt call the local Navy base.

Typical Depth Range:	20-210 feet (~65 m)
Typical Current Conditions:	Moderate to strong
Expertise Required:	Intermediate to advanced
Access:	Boat

About 6 miles (9 km) south of the western side of the Marquesas, a 50-foot (15-m) skeletal lighthouse marks the edge of the drop-off in this area and the northern edge of the Gulf Stream.

Called Cosgrove Shoal after a 19th century captain of the lighthouse tender, this rocky bank runs for miles east and west and is top-notch diving for all activities, probably the closest any of us will get to truly virgin diving areas. Swimming around the lighthouse itself is a treat, because there you will see the legendary monsters of the deep — the Great Barracuda. These barracudas aren't the 4½-foot (1½-m) run-of-the-mill variety; these are the 5-7 foot (1½–2-m) kind. Although there are usually only a half dozen of the big ones, the rest of them (often about 200) are in the standard 3-5-foot (1-2-m) category. No matter how much

The legs of the lighthouse on Cosgrove Shoal are covered with marine life. Here, wrasse and a red-lipped blenny dart among seafans and encrusting sponges that coat the metal structure. (Photo: D. Kincaid.)

The claws of the Florida spider crab are a great delicacy. They are not taken commercially, but divers can fetch their own at Cosgrove Shoals. (Photo: D. Kincaid.)

you know about barracudas being harmless, diving among these will really get your heart beating.

The reef that the lighthouse sits on is a prehistoric dead reef in structure, but it is riddled with coral caves and ledges that contain a wider variety of life than is normally found in the shallow elkhorn and staghorn forests of the Key West reefs. It has colorful crinoids, sponges, sea fans, coral heads, and every variety of deep reef life imaginable. The shallowest part of the reef is close to the lighthouse and about 20 feet (6 m) deep; the slope goes both north to a rubble plain covered with sea fans at about 35 feet (11 m) and out to the south in a gradual slope to 65 or 90 feet (20 or 30 m), where it rises again to about 50 feet (11 m) before finally dropping to 180-210 feet (56-63 m). These deeper areas have occasional bushes of black coral. This is probably the only place in the continental United States where black coral can be found. But because taking or possessing any live coral is against the law, admire its beauty and leave it alone.

The Gulf Stream moves in regularly in this area and when it does, visibility can exceed 150 feet (45 m). The average, though, is about 60-80 feet (18-25 m). On an outgoing tide the current in this area can be severe, so dive upcurrent from your boat, trail a line from the boat with a float on the end, and always leave someone in the boat who knows how to run it in case your anchor breaks loose. Should that happen, the next stop south is Cuba.

Typical Depth Range:	20-120 feet (~36 m)
Typical Current Conditions:	Moderate to strong
Expertise Required:	Intermediate to advanced
Access:	Boat

Marquesas Rock is marked by a large can buoy and is only a mile and a half west of Cosgrove Shoal Lighthouse. There are numerous cracks and crevices in this large rocky plateau, and all around it are ledges that range from a couple of feet (1 m) high to several sheer drops of 40 feet (12 m) or more.

Marine Life. Huge schools of jacks and margates mass here with baitfish, squirrelfish, huge jewfish, and turtles paddling about. Marquesas Rock is another place where truly wild wildlife will occasionally show up — manta rays, sailfish, marlin, sperm whales and, believe it or not, "Jaws," the great white shark — or maybe just a 15-foot (5-m) tiger shark.

A large coral head stands out on the otherwise low relief of the reef at Marquesa Rock. (Photo: D. Kincaid.)

A southern stingray, resting in a sand channel at Marquesa Rock, eyes the photographer suspiciously.(Photo: D. Kincaid.)

Only a half mile (1 km) north of Marquesas Rock is a wrecked vessel from about 1846. There are cannon balls, brass spikes, and rigging lying about, in about 35 feet (11 m) of water on a shifting sand bottom at the end of a rocky ledge. The easiest way to find the wreck is to drag along the ledge behind your boat until you see three large water tanks and the rudder quadrant sticking up. There is also more recent wreckage mixed in with the older one, so it may have been salvaged in the early 1900s.

Again, you are about 30 miles (48 km) from the nearest assistance, so be careful. Have lots of spare parts and a radio that works. The currents here are strong, but they are tidal and thus predictable. The animals are big, as is the sea, and your boat, no matter how well found, is small. It's a lot of water to drink.

6

Safety

This section discusses common hazards and emergency procedures in case of a diving accident. For diagnosis or treatment of serious medical problems, refer to your first aid manual.

Diving Accidents. In case of a diving accident such as a lung overpressure injury (e.g., air embolism, pneumothorax, mediastinal emphysema) or decompression sickness ("bends"), prompt recompression treatment in a chamber may be essential to prevent permanent injury or death.

In case of an accident, remove the victim from the water and place in a supine or flat position. Monitor vital signs and resuscitate or apply CPR if necessary. Administer 100% oxygen, if available. Notify rescue and emergency personnel. On the VHF radio (on most boats), call the U.S. Coast Guard on Channel 16. Call 911 if a phone is available.

Be able to provide rescue and emergency room personnel with the details of the accident or injury as best you can. Include specific details about the victim's dive profile if possible.

The nearest recompression facility is at Mercy Hospital/South Florida Hyperbaric Center at 3633 South Miami Avenue in Miami, Florida 33133. Contact the emergency room at 1-800-662-3637 and ask for the hyperbaric physician on call. Explain the situation. The emergency personnel will arrange transportation. Dade County Fire and Rescue at (305) 285-DIVE (3483) can provide helicopter evacuation.

If rescue squad or ambulance is unavailable, transport victim to the nearest medical facility without delay. In the Upper Keys, Mariners Hospital is located at Milemarker 88.5 Bayside on Plantation Key, (305) 852-9222. In the Middle Keys, Fisherman's Hospital is located in the middle of Marathon, 3301 Overseas Highway, (305) 743-5533. In the Lower Keyes or Key West, Florida Keys Memorial Hospital is located on Stock Island at 5900 Junior College Road, (305) 294-5531.

Emergency contact information can change unpredictably. Readers are advised to check out how to handle an emergency before going on their dive trip.

DAN. The Divers Alert Network (DAN), a non-profit membership association of individuals and organizations sharing a common interest in diving safety operates a 24-hour national hotline, **(919) 684-8111** (collect calls are accepted in an emergency). DAN does *not* maintain any treatment facility nor provide medical care. It does facilitate the entry of an injured diver into a hyperbaric trauma care system by coordinating the efforts of everyone involved in the victim's care.

Additionally, DAN provides diving safety information to members to help prevent accidents. Membership ranges from $25-45 per year, and includes the DAN *Underwater Diving Accident Manual*, which summarizes major diving injuries and outlines procedures for initial management and care of the victim describes symptoms and first aid for the major diving related injuries; a membership card listing diving related symptoms on one side and DAN's emergency and non-emergency phone numbers on the other; decals with DAN's logo and emergency number; and a newsletter, *Alert Diver*, describes diving medicine and safety information in layman's language with articles for professionals, case histories, and medical questions related to diving.DAN membership also includes insurance coverage specifically for dive injuries. Various levels of coverage are available depending upon the membership level. Special memberships for dive stores, dive clubs, and corporations are also available. The DAN manual can be purchased from the Administrative Coordinator, National Diving Alert Network, Duke University Medical Center, Box 3823, Durham, NC 27710.

DAN divides the U.S. into 7 regions, each coordinated by a specialist in diving medicine who has access to the skilled hyperbaric chambers in his region. Non-emergency or information calls are connected to the DAN office and information number, (919) 684-2948. This number can be dialed direct, between 9 am. and 5 pm. Monday-Friday Eastern Standard time. Divers should *not* call DAN for general information on chamber locations. Chamber status changes frequently making this kind of information dangerous if obsolete at the time of an emergency. Instead, divers should contact DAN as soon as a diving emergency is suspected. All divers should have comprehensive medical insurance and check to make sure that hyperbaric treatment and air ambulance services are covered internationally.

Diving is a safe sport and there are very few accidents compared to the number of divers and number of dives made each year. But when the infrequent injury does occur, DAN is ready to help. DAN, originally 100% federally funded, is now largely supported by the diving public. Membership in DAN or purchase of DAN manuals or decals provides divers with useful safety information and provides DAN with necessary operating funds. Donations to DAN are tax deductible as DAN is a legal non-profit public service organization.

Appendix: Dive Shops/Charter Operators

UPPER KEYS

90.5 **Florida Keys Dive Center**
90500 Overseas Highway
P.O. Box 391
Tavernier, Florida 33070
(305) 852-4599; (800) 437-3483

90.3 **Conch Republic Divers, Inc.**
90311 Overseas Highway
Tavernier, Florida 33070
(305) 852-1655; (800) 274-DIVE

87 **Ocean Quest Dive Center**
8700 U.S. Highway 1
Islamorada, Florida 33036
(305) 852-8770; (800) 356-8798

85.9 **Lady Cyana Divers**
P.O. Box 1157
Islamorada, Florida 33036
(305) 664-8717; (800) 221-8717

85.5 **Treasure Divers, Inc.**
85500 Overseas Highway
Islamorada, Florida 33036
(305) 664-5111; (800) 356-9887

84.7 **The Reef Shop & Charter Services**
84771 Overseas Highway
Islamorada, Florida 33036
(305) 664-4385; (800) 741-4385

84.5 **Holiday Isle Dive Center**
P.O. Box 482
Islamorada, Florida 33036
(305) 664-4145; (800) 327-7070

82.0 **Cheeca Divers**
Cheeca Lodge
P.O. Box 1331
Islamorada, Florida 33036
(305) 664-2777; (800) 934-8377

81.5 **World Down Under**
81586 Overseas Highway
Islamorada, Florida 33036
(305) 664-9312; (800) 245-DIVE

79.5 **Bud & Mary's Dive Center**
P.O. Box 1126
Islamorada, Florida 33036
(305) 664-2211; (800) 344-7352

MIDDLE KEYS

61.0 **Ocean Adventures**
Hawk's Cay Resort and Marina
Duck Key, Florida 33050
(305) 743-7000; (800) 432-2242 ext. 3717

54.0 **Abyss Pro Dive Center**
13175 Overseas Highway
Marathon, Florida 33050
(305) 743-2126; (800) 457-0134

53.5 **The Diving Site**
12399 Overseas Highway
Marathon, Florida 33050
(305) 289-1021; (800) 634-3935

53.0 **Capt. Hook's Marina & Dive Center**
11833 Overseas Highway
Marathon, Florida 33050
(305) 743-2444

Camelot Divers
1200 Oceanview Avenue
Marathon, Florida 33050
(305) 743-9369; (800) 441-7991

Tilden's Pro Dive Shop
4650 Overseas Highway
Marathon, Florida 33050
(305) 743-5422; (800) 223-4563

48.0 **Hall's Diving Center**
1994 Overseas Highway
Marathon, Florida 33050
(305) 743-5929; (800) 331-4255

LOWER KEYS

30.5 **Underseas Inc.**
P.O. Box 319
Big Pine Key, Florida 33043
(305) 872-2700; (800) 446-5663

29.5 **Sea Center Dive Shop**
P.O. Box 515
Big Pine Key, Florida 33043
(305) 872-2319

27.5 **Looe Key Reef Resort & Dive Center**
P.O. Box 509
Ramrod Key, Florida 33042
(305) 872-2215; (800) 942-5397

25.0 **Reef Runner Dive Shop**
P.O. Box 96
Summerland Key, Florida 33042
(305) 745-1549

24.5 **Neptune Divers**
Summerland Key, Florida
(305) 745-3365

KEY WEST

Key West Divers, Inc.
U.S. 1 Stock Island
Key West, Florida 33040
(305) 294-7177; (800) 87-DIVER

Key West Pro Dive Shop
1605 North Roosevelt Blvd.
Key West, Florida 33040
(305) 296-3823; (800) 426-0707

Lost Reef Adventures
261 Margaret Street
Lands End Village
Key West, Florida 33040
(305) 296-9737; (800) 633-6833

Reef Raiders Dive Shop
Galleon Marina (or 109 Duval Street)
Key West, Florida 33040
(305) 294-0442; (305) 294-3635

Sea & Sail
Land's End Marina
P.O. Box 6126
Key West, Florida 33041
(305) 294-7280

Southpoint Divers
Key West, Florida 33040
(305) 292-9778; (800) 824-6811

Stars and Stripes
Lands End Marina
P.O. Box 6126
Key West, Florida 33040
(305) 294-PURR; (800) 634-6369

Yankee Freedom
Tortugas Dive Safaris
Land's End Marina
P.O. Box 6126
Key West, Florida 33040
(305) 293-9330; (800) 634-0939

Index

92